THE IDYLLS OF THEOCRITUS

IN ENGLISH VERSE

The Idylls of Theocritus
In English Verse

translated by

W. DOUGLAS P. HILL

SHAKESPEARE HEAD PRESS
ETON, WINDSOR
1959

Printed in Great Britain

41216   PRINTED BY THE DITCHLING PRESS, LTD.,
              DITCHLING, HASSOCKS, SUSSEX.

INTRODUCTION

VERY LITTLE is known for certain about Theocritus. External
evidence suggests that he was the son of Praxagoras and Philinna,
and that he was a native of Syracuse who spent many years in
the island of Cos and visited Alexandria. His poetical activity is
dated in the first three or four decades of the third century B.C.

Internal evidence has nothing to say about his parentage. He
appears to regard himself as a Syracusan (xi. 7 & xxviii. 16), but
his close connection with Cos is manifest. His fruitless appeal to
Hiero II for patronage in Id. xvi and his praise of Ptolemy
Philadelphus in Id. xvii may probably be dated between 275 and
272 B.C.

A full discussion of the subject, purpose and setting of each
Idyll, and of what is known of the life and work of Theocritus,
may be found in A. F. S. Gow's two volumes, comprising an
introduction, text, translation and commentary, published by the
Cambridge University Press (2nd edition, 1952). I must gratefully
acknowledge my debt to his work. He has kindly allowed me to
adopt some very apt epithets and phrases from his prose version
of the poems.

The following Idylls are of doubtful authenticity: viii, ix, xix,
xx, xxi, xxiii, xxv and xxvii.

Three pieces have been added, attributed to a later poet, Bion.
Still less is known about him than about Theocritus. He seems to
have been accounted the leading poet of his day, but even his
date is uncertain.

THE SONG OF THYRSIS

Thyrsis

How sweet the whisper of yon spring-fed pine;
   Sweet, too, O goatherd, are thy melodies,
   And only Pan can wrest from thee the prize.
If his the hornéd goat, the she-goat thine;
   Choose he the she-goat, thine the kid, whose meat,
   Ere it be milked, is sweet.

Goatherd

Sweeter thy song, O shepherd, than the voice
   Of the tumbling stream that plashes from the rocks;
   And if the Muses from among the flocks
Choose as their prize the ewe, then shall thy choice
   Be the fat lamb; if theirs the lamb, the ewe,
   Thyrsis, shall be thy due.

Thyrsis

Now, in the Nymphs' name, sit thee down and play,
O goatherd, where the tamarisks' array
Shelters the sloping knoll, and I'll
Pasture thy goats the while.

Goatherd

Nay, shepherd, nay; we may not pipe at noon.
This is the hour when Pan, the hunter, wearied,
Rests from the chase; we fear to break his rest,
So quickly is he vexed, so choleric.
But thou, O Thyrsis, whose perpetual theme
Is Daphnis' woe, skilled master in the art
Of pastoral song, come hither; here we'll sit
Beneath the elm, where shepherds sit and oaks

Spread their broad boughs, and old Priapus stands
To face us 'mid the springs; and if thou sing
As once when Libyan Chromis matched his song
With thine, then for a guerdon may'st thou milk
Three times a goat that gives twin kids to drink
Yet fills two pails beside; and a deep cup
I'll give thee, coated with sweet wax, new-made,
Still fragrant from the graving-knife, two-handled.
Above, along the rim, the ivy-tendril
Trails sinuous, rejoicing in its fruit,
Gold clustered berries laid between the leaves.
Within, a woman, cloaked and circleted,
Fair as some god might fashion, stands enwrought,
While at her side two lovers vie in speech
To win her favour, fair with flowing locks.
Now this one speaks, now that; and yet their words
Touch not her heart; but now she looks on one
And smiles, now turns her thought to heed the other;
Both toil in vain, love-stricken, hollow-eyed.
And next engraved an aged fisherman
Stands on a rugged rock and eagerly
Draws close his heavy net to make a cast;
Strongly he toils, till all about his neck
Stand out the sinews—grey, wave-worn and old;
Yet, as he labours, seems his strength a boy's.
Hard by, a carven vineyard, where the vines
Droop with empurpled clusters, and a child
Sits idly on a loose stone wall to guard
The ripening grapes; and see, two wily foxes
Lurk near, one ravaging the grapes and one
Intent, uncaught, to steal the poor lad's bread
From his unguarded wallet; but the child,
Gathering asphodel and rush to plait
A pretty cricket-cage, cares naught for vines
Or wallet—all his joy is in his task.

2

And all about the cup the pliant stems
Of the acanthus spread their leaves—a marvel
To please a goatherd's eyes and dazzle thine!
And though I paid the boatman of Calydna
One great white cheese, yea, and a goat thereto,
It lies unsullied yet, nor has it touched
These lips of mine. Now, friend, but sing that song,
That lovely song, and with right willingness
Will I delight thee with this wondrous gift.
'Tis truth I speak; come now, good sir, thy song!
Sing while thou may'st; thou can'st not carry hence
Thy songs to Hades, where is no remembrance!

Thyrsis
Begin, ye Muses dear, begin the pastoral song!

Thyrsis of Etna am I and the voice of Thyrsis is sweet.
　Where were ye, Nymphs, where were ye when love-stricken
　　　　　　　　　　　Daphnis was wasting?
Were the fair valleys of Pindus or Peneius your retreat?
　For surely ye were not found where the stream of Anapus
　　　　　　　　　　　was hasting,
Nor on the peak of Etna's mountain, your wonted seat,
Nor by the holy river of Acis at Etna's feet.

　Begin, ye Muses dear, begin the pastoral song!

Howled wolves, and jackals howled, lamenting;
　And from the woods the lion crept and shed
　Tears, bitter tears, for Daphnis dead!

　Begin, ye Muses dear, begin the pastoral song!

About his feet stood cows and heifers weeping,
And calves and bulls, sorrowful vigil keeping.

3

Begin, ye Muses dear, begin the pastoral song!

First from the hill came Hermes: 'Ah, what love,'
He cried, 'dear Daphnis, hath such power to move
   Thee to this dire tormenting?'

   Begin, ye Muses dear, begin the pastoral song!

The neatherds came, shepherds and goatherds, crying,
   'What ails thee, Daphnis?' Old Priapus said,
'Poor wretch, why thus for bootless love art dying?
   Knowest thou not by every fount and glade

   Begin, ye Muses dear, begin the pastoral song!

The maiden seeks thee, backward lover, straying?
   Once oxherd, now a goatherd's thy desires,
   Who sees the nannies sporting with their sires
And yearns to be a goat and join their playing!

   Begin, ye Muses dear, begin the pastoral song!

So thou, who seest the maidens' laughter blending
   With merry dance, weepest to take no part!'
   So spake his friends, but Daphnis steeled his heart
Silent, and bore his love to the bitter ending.

   Begin, ye Muses, once again the pastoral song!

Came too the Cyprian goddess, smiling sweetly,
   A secret smile that masked an inner rage:
   'Ah, Daphnis, Love to o'erthrow didst thou engage,
And hath not cruel Love o'erthrown thee featly?'

   Begin, ye Muses, once again the pastoral song!

4

Then answered Daphnis, 'Cypris hard to move,
  Wrathful, abhorréd in the world of men,
  Deemest thou this my sunset? Know thou then
Sorely in Hades will I torture Love!

    Begin, ye Muses, once again the pastoral song!

Ha! Cypris and the neatherd! What a tale!
  Get thee to Ida! To Anchises hie;
  There by the hives hum bees melodiously
And grow strong oaks and scented galingale!

    Begin, ye Muses, once again the pastoral song!

Forget not thou Adonis, ripe and fair,
Shepherd and hunter, slayer of the hare!

    Begin, ye Muses, once again the pastoral song!

Go, challenge Diomede once more and say,
"Daphnis is vanquished; come, be slain or slay!"

    Begin, ye Muses, once again the pastoral song!

Farewell, ye wolves and jackals! Bears of the hills,
  Farewell! No more to thicket, grove or dell
  Comes Daphnis; Arethusa, fare thee well,
And Thybris' beauteous down-cascading rills!

    Begin, ye Muses, once again the pastoral song!

Daphnis am I that pastured here my kine;
The bulls and calves I watered here were mine.

    Begin, ye Muses, once again the pastoral song!

Come down, O Pan, down from Lycaeus' height
    Or mighty Maenalus to Sicily;
    Leave thou the lofty peak of Helice
And Lycaon's son's high tomb, the gods' delight!

    Cease now, ye Muses, cease the pastoral song!

Come now, my lord, and take this scented reed,
    With honeyed wax compacted, and around
    Its elegant lip securely wrapped and bound;
I go to Hades; thus hath Love decreed!

    Cease now, ye Muses, cease the pastoral song!

Now, thorns, bear violets; bear violets now
Ye brambles! Let the fair narcissus grow
On the juniper, and on the pine the pear!
Now let the hunted stag the fierce hounds tear!
Now from the mountains let the owls cry vying
With Philomela's song! Daphnis is dying!'

    Cease now, ye Muses, cease the pastoral song!

Silent he fell, and though the Cyprian strove
    To raise him up, stern Fate had snapped the thread
    Assigned; the waters closed o'er Daphnis' head,
The darling of the Nymphs, the Muses' love.

    Cease now, ye Muses, cease the pastoral song!

    Give me the prize; my song is done;
    I'll milk the goat, and from the bowl
    To the blest Nine of Helicon
    Pour due libation.
    Farewell, ye Muses, and another day
    I'll sing you a yet sweeter lay!

6

Goatherd

Honeyed thy lips; on honey feed
  And honeycomb, and may the sweet
  Figs of Aegilia be thy meat!
    For verily thy song outvies
    The tuneful cricket's melodies.
Take now the cup that is thy meed!
  How sweet its smell,
  As if the Hours' own well
  Had washed it! Come, Cissaetha, now,
  And, Thyrsis, milk her thou!
A truce, ye nannies, to your revelries,
Lest, where he lies,
The he-goat stir himself and rise!

IDYLL II

THE SORCERESS

Where are my bay-leaves? Bring them, Thestylis,
And all that is
Of magic power, and with fine crimson wool
Wreathe thou the bowl,
That I with witch's spell may bind my love,
So hard to move!

My love? Ah, cruel wretch, eleven days
And still he stays!
No knock at the door! Whether I live or die
His perfidy
Recks not; Love and the Cyprian have inclined
His fickle mind
To seek some rival maiden, while I wait
Scorned, desolate!

7

Tomorrow to the wrestling-school I'll hie,
Face him and cry,
'Why treat my suit with this ungallant scorn,
Leave me forlorn?'
Today I'll draw him, bound to my desire,
With potent fire!

Shine bright, O Moon! I'll sing my quiet song
And plead my wrong
To thee and that grim sorceress of Hell,
Whose presence fell
Sets the dogs howling as they watch her tread
Over the dead,
Over the graves and the blood's dark red sea!
O Hecate!
Hail, goddess! Now do thou my spells attend
Unto the end,
And on my magic drugs in this dread hour
Bestow such power
As wielded once those old enchantresses
Circe, Medea and Perimede of the golden tresses!

Draw to my house, O Wheel, the man I love!

Barley smoulders on the flame!
Strew the groats and name his name!
Mock me not, poor coward maid;
Thy wandering fancy whither strayed?
Haste and add this spell thereto,
'Bones of Delphis here I strew!'

Draw to my house, O Wheel, the man I love!

Delphis scorns me; so in turn
I these crackling bay-leaves burn;

Sudden catch and vanish quite;
Not an ash be left in sight!
Even as this burning bay
Flesh of Delphis waste away!

Draw to my house, O Wheel, the man I love!

Burn, bran! Thou canst, O Artemis,
Burst Hades' gates and all that is
Most stubborn; hark, the town-dogs greet,
Howling where the three roads meet,
The advancing goddess! Ere she pass,
Clang, Thestylis, the gong of brass!

Draw to my house, O Wheel, the man I love!

Calm lies the sea, the breezes rest;
Unquiet the torment in my breast!
This wretched heart, by pain untaught,
Spite of the wrongs my love hath wrought,
Yet burns with a consuming flame—
Nor wife nor maid, a thing of shame!

Draw to my house, O Wheel, the man I love!

Goddess, aid! On thee I call!
As I melt this waxen ball,
So be Myndian Delphis burned!
As, by Aphrodite turned,
Whirls this rhomb with brazen roar,
May he turn about my door!

Draw to my house, O Wheel, the man I love!

Thrice cry I, Lady Hecate,

9

And thrice libation pour to thee!
As Theseus on the isle that morn
Left fair-tressed Ariadne lorn
And sailed away, e'en so may he
Leave his new love and turn to me!

Draw to my house, O Wheel, the man I love!

Foals and mares of fleetest foot
Race to seek this milky root,
Crazed with longing on the wold
Of Arcady; may I behold
Delphis from the wrestling flee,
Maddened, yearning, home to me!

Draw to my house, O Wheel, the man I love!

This fringe that Delphis' mantle shed
With jealous hands I take and shred
And cast into the cruel fire
To burn! Ah, torturing desire,
Why like some fen-bred leech dost drain
My storm-tossed heart of all but pain?

Draw to my house, O Wheel, the man I love!

Venomed lizard next I'll bray
For his morning draught! Away!
O'er his threshold kneading throw
Magic herbs and mutter low,
While black night conceals thy deed,
'Bones of Delphis here I knead!'

Draw to my house, O Wheel, the man I love!

Alas, I am alone! How now lament
    Or seek the source of this accursed love?
'Twas on the day Eubulus' daughter went
    As basket-bearer to the sacred grove
Of Artemis, where many a savage beast—
A lioness too—came proud to grace her feast.

    Mark, Lady Moon, whence sprang this hapless love!

A Thracian dame, now dead, dwelt by my home,
    Theumaridas's nurse; with urgency
She prayed me view the pageant, crying, 'Come,
    O come!' and I consented—woe is me!
So in my silken gown myself I dressed,
With Clearista's shawl about my breast.

    Mark, Lady Moon, whence sprang this hapless love!

Scarce had we halved our road, by Lycon's land,
    When on the selfsame pathway met our eyes
Delphis and Eudamippus, hand in hand;
    Golden their beards, fairer than helichryse,
Fresh from the wrestling-bout, their breasts agleam,
Brighter, Selene, than thy brightest beam.

    Mark, Lady Moon, whence sprang this hapless love!

I saw, and madness seized me, and I burned
    With passionate fire, unhappy heart, aglow.
Faded my erstwhile beauty; I returned—
    I know not how—no thought for pomp or show.
A violent ague shook me; on my bed
Ten days, ten nights I lay uncomforted.

    Mark, Lady Moon, whence sprang this hapless love!

Pale grew my face, and day by day my hair
    Fell from my head, and now my frame was nought
But bones and skin; ah, then in dull despair
    The homes of witch and sorceress I sought
And hags expert in magic pharmacy,
But all in vain; and time went flying by.

Mark, Lady Moon, whence sprang this hapless love!

'Come, Thestylis,' I cried, 'I'll tell thee all!
    Find me some cure for this my dolorous state.
The Myndian Delphis holds my heart in thrall;
    There is no healing; nay, go haunt the gate
Of Timagetus' school, where wrestlers sport;
There Delphis loves to sit, that his resort.

Mark, Lady Moon, whence sprang this hapless love!

Find him apart from others; nod thy head;
    Whisper "Simaetha calls thee" secretly.'
So spake I, and she went and hither led
    Delphis sleek-limbed and brought him here to me.
And I no sooner knew that he had come
Light-foot across the threshold of my home—

Mark, Lady Moon, whence sprang this hapless love!

Than I turned cold, colder than snow, and sweat
    Bedewed my brow, nor could my numb lips move
To speak, nay, not so much as babes that fret,
    Crying in sleep upon their mothers' love.
I could not stir, nor could my limbs relax;
Stiff like a doll I stood, rigid as wax.

Mark, Lady Moon, whence sprang this hapless love!

Then, glancing at my face, he fixed his eyes
    (Untrue, untrue) upon the ground and spake,
Seated upon my couch in loving wise,
    'Truly, Simaetha, did thy call o'ertake
My instant coming by as little space
As I outstripped Philinus in the race!

    Mark, Lady Moon, whence sprang this hapless love!

I would have come—by Love's sweet self I swear—
    At early dusk with friends in company,
Borne with me Dionysus' apples, fair
    Love-tokens, leaves of the white poplar tree,
Heracles' holy plant, upon my brow,
With crimson bands entwined, to make my vow!

    Mark, Lady Moon, whence sprang this hapless love!

And had I found thee kind, Oh then what bliss!
    No stripling nimbler, none more fair than I!
And had these lips pressed with a lover's kiss
    Thy lips, I should have dreamed in ecstasy!
But hadst thou barred the door and said me nay,
Then truly axe and torch had forced my way!

    Mark, Lady Moon, whence sprang this hapless love!

But no; when near consumed by love's hot flame,
    That oft burns fiercer than Hephaestus' fire
On Lipara, thou called'st me and I came,
    Snatched from the burning by thy sweet desire!
Thanks to thee, Cyprian, for thy clemency,
And thanks, most gracious mistress, thanks to thee!

    Mark, Lady Moon, whence sprang this hapless love!

'Tis Love, whose passionate madness drives a bride,
  Reckless, to leave her husband's warm embrace!'
So spake he, and I drew him to my side;
  Body to body, face to burning face,
Sweetly we whispered; credulous I lent
My ear; we twain found love's accomplishment.

Such is my tale, dear Moon; till late
No shadow fell upon our love;
Only today, when rosy Dawn,
Borne by swift steeds from Ocean, climbed
The sky, Philista's mother came
(Philista plays the flute) and told
How Delphis loved another—whom
She knew not—only this, that oft
He raised a cup of wine unmixed
And toasted Love; then hot-foot ran
To wreathe his loved one's gate with flowers.

That was the tale my gossip told
And I believe her; thrice a day,
Nay, four times formerly he'd come
To visit me and ofttimes leave
His oil-flask in my keeping; now
Eleven weary days have passed
And not a sight of him! 'Tis true,
I am forgot; some new delight
Has charmed remembrance from his heart!

Now with my magic, by the Fates,
I'll bind him! An he vex me still,
He'll beat upon the gate of Hell!
My chest holds yet such evil drugs
Whose potency I learnt, O Queen,
From an Assyrian sorcerer.

But now farewell, O Lady; turn
Thy steeds towards Ocean; I shall bear,
As I have borne, my longing still.
Moon on thy shining throne, farewell!
Farewell, ye stars, whose quiet light
Follows the car of tranquil Night!

IDYLL III

SERENADE

I go Amaryllis's charms to praise
   While Tityrus herds my goats on the hill.
Friend Tityrus, guard them while they graze
   And water them down by the rill,
Alert
Lest the tawny Libyan do thee hurt!

O charming Amaryllis, why no more
   Peep'st from thy cave to greet thy love
      And call him in?
Is he then uglier than of yore—
   Snub nose? Projecting chin?
Say, dost thou hate me? Thou wilt move
   Thy wounded love to hanging! See,
      I've brought ten apples here for thee
From that same grove
   Where thou didst bid me pluck them, and again
      I'll bring thee more! Oh, but this pain
         Tortures my heart!
Ah, would I were yon buzzing bee!
   I'd pierce the ivy and the fern
      That hide thy cave and dart
Through their green veil to thee!

And now I learn
Grievous a god is Love; a lioness
Surely hath suckled him with ruthlessness
In some wild forest; for his smouldering fire
Torments my very bones with vain desire!

O maiden dark of brow,
    Whose least glance charms,
But with a heart of stone, come now,
    Come to my arms,
That I may know thy kisses;
For though they be but cold, there sweetest bliss is!

I wear a wreath of ivy twined
    With rose and fragrant celery;
    I wear it, dear, for thee.
But, Amaryllis, if thou be not kind,
    I'll shred it into fragments! What,
Oh what will stay my misery?
    Thou hearkenest not!

I'll strip my cloak and leap into the sea
    Where fisher Olpis watches from the bluff
For tunny; if I drown, then that will be
Sweet news for thee!
    That is enough!

An omen lately taught me
The truth when I bethought me
    Did Amaryllis love me, did she hate?
Did love-in-absence' petal
On my smooth forearm settle?
    It clung not—withered—and I knew my fate!

Agroeo too, who by the sieve speaks sooth,

Was near me, cutting grass, and told me truth:
  'Thy heart,' she said, 'is wholly hers, but she
  Makes no account of thee.'

Two kids has the nanny I'm keeping for thee
Which Mermnon's dark handmaid doth covet, and see!
  If she begs it again, I'll give it her yet,
  Since thou playest ever the arch coquette!

My right eye is twitching! Is it a sign
  I shall see her anon? I'll sing her a song
As I stand beneath yon pine;
  And it may be ere long
She'll relent and prove
That her heart can be melted by love!

Song

Hear how Hippomenes planned
  To win Atalanta perforce;
With golden apples in his hand
  He ran his course;
And Atalanta saw, and frenzy drove
Her headlong down into the depths of love.

Melampus the seer, when Bias wooed,
  The stolen kine to Pylus brought
From Othrys, and in gratitude
  For the great grace thus wrought
The king gave lovely Peiro to be wed
To Bias, and anon their marriage-bed
  Was blessed with wise Alphesiboea.

When on the hills Adonis fed his sheep,
  Fair Cytherea
Even in his last eternal sleep,

By love's sweet frenzy still possessed,
Clasped the dear shepherd to her breast.

Happy I deem Endymion
  Who sleeps the sleep unturning,
And happy too Iasion
  For Ceres' favour burning;
And what his lot,
Profane, ye augur not!

That is my song; no more I sing.
  My brain's afire! Thou carest not!
    Here where I fall
    The wolves shall maul
My body in their ravening!
    And sweeter far to thee
    Than honeycomb may be
My wretched lot!

IDYLL IV

THE HERDSMEN

Battus   Say, Corydon, are these Philondas' cows?
Corydon No, Aegon bade me graze them.
B.   I'll be sworn
You milk them of an evening on the sly!
C.   Indeed I don't! The old man watches me
And puts the calves beneath their dams himself.
B.   And where's the master herdsman, Aegon, gone?
C.   Haven't you heard? Milon has hauled him off
To the Olympic games.
B.   What, Aegon box?
I'll warrant it's the first time he's seen oil!

C.	They say he's just as strong as Heracles.
B.	Yes, and my mother says that I can box Better than Polydeuces!
C.	Well, he's gone With a pickaxe for his training, and for food A score of sheep.
B.	If Milon could persuade Aegon to box, he could persuade the wolves Run rabid through the flocks!
C.	D'you hear them low? The heifers miss their master.
B.	Yes, poor beasts! They've got a scurvy herdsman!
C.	Poor indeed! They're off their feed.
B.	Just look at that thin calf; She's skin and bones; what does she get to eat? Dewdrops, like the cicada?
C.	Dewdrops? No! I graze her by Aesarus; there she chews Soft hay, a luscious bundle; and at times She gambols on Latymnum in the shade.
B.	That bull—the ruddy one—he's thin; God grant Those scoundrels, Lampriadas' deme, may find Just such another when they sacrifice To Hera!
C.	Yet I drive him to the marsh, To Physcus' fields, Neaethus too, and there There's plenty of good feed for such as he— Restharrow, fleabane and sweet-scented balm.
B.	Aegon, you wretch, your cows will pine and die, And all because you've set your cursèd heart On victory! The pipe you made yourself Lies mildewed!

C.   By the Nymphs, it's no such thing!
He left the pipe to me when he went off
To Pisa; and what's more, I'd have you know
I'm no mean player! Glauce's, Pyrrhus' airs
I can strike up, or sing our Croton's praise—
'O beautiful Zacynthus!' or again
Lacinian Hera's shrine that fronts the dawn.
That was where boxer Aegon wolfed the loaves,
Full eighty of them, all alone, and caught
The bull by the hoof and dragged it down the hill
As a gift to Amaryllis; how he laughed
To hear the women screaming!

B.   Dead, alas,
My lovely Amaryllis! You alone
Live in our memory; we'll not forget!
I loved you dying as I love my goats;
O heartless power that sways my destiny!

C.   Cheer up, friend Battus; things may take a turn
Tomorrow; while there's life, there's hope; the dead
Have none; bright sky today and rain tomorrow;
It's as God wills.

B.   I'm not downhearted; look,
The calves are nibbling olive-shoots below!
Come, drive them up, the brutes!

C.   Lepargus, hi!
Hi there, Cymaetha! Up! Are you deaf? Clear out
Or I'll come and drub you—yes, by Pan, I will!
Just look, she's back again! Oh for a club,
A crooked one, to whack you with, you brute!

B.   O Corydon, look here; I've got a thorn
Stuck just below my ankle; how they grow,
These spindle-thorns! A plague upon this heifer!
It pricked me as I gaped at her; d'you see it?

C.   Yes, yes, I've got it in my nails, and here's
The thorn itself.

20

B.	Why, what a tiny wound
	To overcome a great big man like me!
C.	Well, Battus, don't walk barefoot on the hills
	Where thorns and brambles flourish.
B.	Tell me now,
	Is the old fool still chasing, Corydon,
	That dark-browed girl he fell in love with?
C.	Yes,
	Indeed he is, my friend! The other day
	I happened on him by the byre, and phew!
	Wasn't he going it!
B.	Well, good luck to him,
	Dirty old man! That sort's about a match
	For Satyrs, yes, and scraggy goat-legged Pans!

IDYLL V

GOATHERD AND SHEPHERD

Comatas	Hey there, my goats, keep out of the way
	Of that shepherd of Sybaris! Yesterday
	He stole my goatskin!
Lacon	Psst, my lambs,
	Away from the spring! Or don't you see
	Comatas, the fellow who stole my pipe?
C.	Your pipe indeed! Where got you a pipe,
	Sibyrtas' slave? Enough for you
	An oaten whistle, and Corydon too,
	To toot your tunes on!
L.	The very same pipe
	That Lycon gave me, Mister Free!
	And as for your skin, how could Lacon steal
	Such a thing when your master, Eumarus, has none
	To wrap himself in of a night?

C.	The one

C.   The one
That Crocylus gave me, the dappled skin
When he slew the goat to the Nymphs, and you—
You envied my luck at the time, and now
You've stripped me at last and left me bare!

L.   By Pan of the Shore, Calaethis' son
Never filched your cloak! If I did, good sir,
May I lose my wits and run and leap
Into the Crathis from yonder steep!

C.   By the Nymphs of the Lake—and may they be
Gracious and kind—Comatas swears
He never laid hands on your pipe, good sir!

L.   May the sorrows of Daphnis fall on me
If ever I trust you! But come, if you care
To wager a kid—not much to ask—
I'll match you with song till you cry 'Enough!'

C.   The pig and Athene! There's the kid;
So stake a fat lamb yourself.

L.   You fox!
D'you call that fair? Shear hair for wool?
Who wants to milk a beastly bitch
Instead of a goat with a firstling kid?

C.   Why, you, I suppose, if you're so dead sure
Of beating your neighbour—the buzz of a wasp
To match a cicada's song! Well, look,
If you fancy the kid isn't fair, then take
The billy-goat here for a stake. Start up!

L.   What's all the hurry? You're not on fire!
Come and sit in the shade where the olive grows
And trees spread their branches; it's sweeter to sing
On a grassy couch where the crickets chirp
And water drips cool.

C.   No hurry, I grant.
What worries me's this, that a boy like you
Whom I taught as a child should have the nerve

	To challenge your teacher. Well, that's the fruit
	That kindness bears—you rear a pup,
	Or a wolf-cub rather, to eat you up!
L.	You envious beast, I'm not aware
	That I ever learnt anything good from you!
C.	What a memory!
L.	Curse on your corpse! Come here,

L.　　　　　　　　　　　Curse on your corpse! Come here,
And I'll see that you never sing songs again!

C.　No. I'll not come there; there are oak-trees here
And galingale too, and the murmur of bees
Round the hives is sweet; from a couple of springs
There flows cool water, and on the trees
The birds are twittering; as for your shade,
It's nothing to mine! And the pine above
Is dropping its cones.

L.　　　　　　　　　　　Just come over here
And you'll tread on fleeces soft as sleep,
I swear it, and lambskins. Faugh! The stink
Of your goatskins there! It's worse than yours!
I'll set for the Nymphs a bowl of milk,
A great big bowl of the whitest milk,
And another of sweetest oil.

C.　　　　　　　　　　　But you,
If only you come over here, shall tread
On blossoming pennyroyal and fern;
And as for your lambskins, here you'll lie
On the skins of goats four times as soft.
I'll set eight pails of milk for Pan,
Eight bowls of honeycomb too.

L.　　　　　　　　　　　Very well,
Compete from there and sing your song!
Tread your own ground; you can keep your oaks!
But who shall be judge? I'd like to see
Lycopas the oxherd coming this way.

C.　Lycopas? I don't want him; but look,

There's a woodman cutting the heath near you.
Let's give him a shout; it's Morson.

L.   Right!
Let's shout!

C.   You call him!

L.   Hi there, friend!
Just come for a moment and listen to us.
There's a match on between us; we want to decide
Which is the better at country songs.
Now, Morson my friend, be impartial to both;
Don't judge me too kindly, and don't favour *him*.

C.   Yes, Morson, don't favour Comatas or *him*!
Sibyrtas of Thurii owns this flock;
Eumarus of Sybaris owns these goats.

L.   Heaven help you, who asked you who owned the flock,
Sibyrtas or I? What a talker you are!

C.   I'm telling the truth, good man, no boasts;
It's you that are quarrelsome!

L.   That's enough;
If you've anything more to say, say on;
But let friend Morson get back to town
Alive, Comatas, you garrulous fool!

THE CONTEST

Comatas Two goats have I slain to the Muses and none can deny,
Though Daphnis the singer is dear to them, dearer am I.

Lacon Yes, yes, and I'm dear to Apollo, and now for his feast,
The autumn Carnea, I'm feeding a fine fat beast.

C.   Nigh all of the nannies I milk have twin kids, and
                                        there eyes
Me the maiden: 'Poor fellow, alone in thy milking?'
                                        she cries.

24

L.   Oh, that's a mere nothing! I, Lacon, fill baskets with
cheese,
Near twenty, and tumble my love on the flowery leas.

C.   Clearista throws apples to tease me driving my herds,
Love-fruit for Comatas, and sweet are her notes as a
bird's.

L.   When Cratidas meets me, his shepherd, with gentle
delight,
I'm maddened; and see, how the locks on his neck
wave bright!

C.   What are briar or anemone? Naught to compare with
the rose
That deep in its bed by the wall of the garden blows.

L.   Wild apple and acorn! Can one with the other
compete?
The rind of the acorn is thin, but the apple is sweet.

C.   And soon for a gift to my darling I'll catch her a dove,
Where it roosts unaware in the juniper, token of love.

L.   But I to my Cratidas freely, as soon as I shear
The black ewe, shall be giving the fleece as a soft
cloak to wear.

C.   Come away from the olives, my kids; you may graze
to your fill
Where the tamarisks grow, up here on the slope of the
hill.

L.   Away from the oak there, Cinaetha! Hi, Conarus too!
Phalarus is here to the east; come and feed with him you!

C. An exquisite bowl, by the hand of Praxiteles graved,
    And a cypress-wood pail for my darling I've stored up
    and saved.

L. For my boy there's a dog that is death to the wolves
    and a shield
    To the flock; with its aid he shall harry the beasts of
    the field.

C. O ye locusts that hopping leap over our fences and fly,
    Do no harm to my vineyard; the grapes on the branches
    are dry.

L. As I am provoking the goatherd with music and song,
    You crickets keep teasing the reapers all day long.

C. A plague on the foxes, the bushy-tailed vermin, that
    creep
    To plunder the vines in the evening when Micon's
    asleep!

L. And a plague on the beetles that ravish Philondas's
    trees
    And nibble his figs, and are off, borne swift on the
    breeze!

C. I know someone who's losing his temper! D'you hear
    him rave?
    Run, Morson, and gather you squills from an old hag's
    grave!

L. And I know a fellow I'm galling—you see it, I'm sure;
    Go quick to the Haleis, dig cyclamen root for a cure!

C. May Himera's water be milk, and, Crathis, thy flow

Blush purple with wine, and fruit on thy reeds hang
low!

L. Let Sybaris' stream flow with honey for me, and at
dawn
May my maid in her pail find no water, but honeycomb
drawn!

C. They feed on moon-clover, my goats, and on mastich
they tread;
Goatwort is their pasture, arbutus their evergreen bed!

L. And there browse my sheep where the balm bee-
haunted grows,
And lush on the rocks flowers the cistus as red as the
rose.

C. I love not Alcippa; 'twere thankless an ingrate to love;
She kissed me not, caught not my ears, when I gave
her a dove.

L. But dearly Eumedes I love; when I gave him a reed,
His embraces were sweet and his kisses were charming
indeed.

C. How can jays vie with nightingales, hoopoes with
swans? It's not right!
But Lacon, you quarrelsome fool, why so keen on a
fight?

Morson Have done now, shepherd; the prize I declare
To be yours, Comatas; sacrifice
Your lamb to the Nymphs, and be sure to spare
Morson a fine fat slice.

Comatas I'll do it, by Pan! Now, you kids of my flock,
Give a gleeful snort, for I'm able to mock
Poor Lacon, the shepherd! I've won the prize
And to please my flock I'll leap to the skies!
Cheer up, my goats! Tomorrow I'll take
You all to be washed in Sybaris' lake!

IDYLL VI

DAMOETAS AND DAPHNIS

Hard by a spring, when the summer noon was hot,
   Damoetas, on whose cheek the golden down was lying,
And Daphnis, bearded youth, had gathered to one spot
   Their common herd, Aratus; there in friendly vying
They sat and sang, and Daphnis, challenging,
     Was first to sing.

'See, Polyphemus, see where Galatea
   With apples pelts thy flocks,
   Taunts thee and mocks,
Calling thee love-accurst and rustic goatherd!

'Seated aloof—no eye for her—thou pipest,
   Pipest a tuneful strain,
   And once again a rain
Of apples showers upon the faithful dog

'That guards thy sheep! Hear how she barks,
   Coursing upon the strand,
   Where on the murmuring sand
Wash and retreat the gentle waves of ocean,
   Reflecting in their mirror
Her restless motion.

'Heed lest thy sheep-dog spring on Galatea
    To tear her lovely ankles as the maiden
        Moves from the sea!
        Wanton, she wooeth thee,
        E'en from so far, and turns to flee

'Light as the down that trembles on the thistle
    And flies upon the wind, sun-dried;
        No wile untried,
She flees the lover and pursues the loveless!

'Yea, Polyphemus, oft-times love is blind,
And to his seeming foul is fair and kind!'

So Daphnis sang; Damoetas, answering,
Piped a sweet prelude and began to sing:

'Nay, but, by Pan, I spied her casting apples
With my one eye—sweet eye, long may it serve me,
Spite of the prophet! Blinded be his own eyes!
        Blinded his children's!

'See how I tease her, teasing for her teasing,
Feign that I heed her not, have wed another!
Oh then with what mad jealousy and frenzy,
        Paean be witness,

'Eyes she my flocks and caves! When erst I wooed her,
Soft on her lap my dog would lay her muzzle,
Whining for notice; now my trusty guardian
        Barks at my bidding.

'And though she send a messenger to court me,
Barred will my cave-door stand until she promise
She and none else our marriage-bed will fashion
        Here on the island.

'Truly my form is fair, though men malign me;
Once when the sea's calm surface made a mirror,
Fair showed my beard and fair my eye, reflected;
    Parian marble

'Scarce could compete, I swear it, with the whiteness
Of my white teeth! Then, to avert disaster,
Thrice did I spit, as the old witch had taught me,
    Into my bosom.'

So sang Damoetas, and embracing Daphnis
Gave him a pipe, and Daphnis gave Damoetas
    A pretty flute and straight began to play
        Upon the reed; and to his lip
Damoetas set his flute harmoniously.
        Then to the melody the calves gan skip
    In the soft hay.
Invincible were both in song, though neither
    Had won the day.

IDYLL VII

HARVEST FESTIVAL

    There was a day when Eucritus and I—
    Amyntas too was with us—left the town
    To seek the Haleis and Demeter's shrine,
    Where Phrasidamus and Antigenes,
    Sons of Lycopeus, were offering
    The first-fruits of the harvest, noble pair
    Of Clytia's line and Chalcon's, from whose foot,
    When his firm knee pressed hard upon the rock,
    Sprang the Burina fount; and by that spring
    Poplars and elms arched their green foliage,
    Luxuriant, to weave a floor of shade.

30

But when not half our way was done, nor yet
Brasilas' tomb was viewed, by the Muses' grace
We met a traveller, a Cydonian;
Lycidas was he named, a worthy man,
A goatherd; nor could any fail to mark
He was a goatherd; for the tawny hide
Of a rough shaggy goat fell mantlewise,
Reeking of rennet, from his shoulders; girt
With a broad belt, an old worn tunic hid
His breast; in his right hand a crooked club
He grasped, cut from wild olive; and he spoke
With twinkling eye, smiling a quiet smile,
While laughter trembled on his lip: 'How now?
Whither dost bend thy steps, Simichidas,
In the noontide heat, when even the lizard sleeps
In the cool of the crannied wall, and crested larks
Stir not abroad? Dost speed to a banqueting
Unbidden, or some townsman's winepress? See
How every pebble in thy hasty path
Spurned by thy shoes, flies singing!'
                                        I replied,
'Friend Lycidas, all say thou hast no match
At piping; herdsmen, reapers yield to thee;
It glads my heart to hear it, yet methinks
I am thine equal. But we travel now
To a harvest-festival; good friends of mine
Are offering first-fruits of their winnowed grain
To the fair-robed Goddess, by whose bounteous hand
Their floor is heaped with barley. Come, the way,
The day, are ours to share; let us sing songs,
Sing country songs, that each may profit each.
Mine too is a melodious voice; I too
Am called the best of singers; though, by Zeus,
I scarce can claim the title, for I hold
Not yet with Samian Sicelidas

31

Nor with Philetas can I match my song,
A frog to match cicadas!'
                              So I spake
With purpose, and the goatherd made reply,
Pleasantly laughing:
                     'Earn my stick! for Zeus
Hath fashioned thee a sprig compact of truth!
I hate the builder whose ambitious hand
Would raise his house to match the loftiest peak
Of Mount Oromedon; I hate those too,
Cocks of the Muses, whose vain crowing strives
To vie with the Chian bard! But come, my friend,
Let us forthwith begin our pastoral songs,
And I, Simichidas—see if it please,
This ode I late composed upon the hill:

                  Lycidas sings
Fair may thy voyage to Mitylene be,
Ageanax, when on the stormy sea
Orion rests, and in the evening sky
The Kids are rising, and the waves run high,
    Driven before the wind,
    So thou be kind
And save from Aphrodite's fire
Lycidas, scorched by fierce desire!

Halcyons, lay to rest the billowy deep,
The south wind and the east, that stirs from sleep
Weed in the depths remote—halcyons, they
Whom the green Nereids love, and all who prey
    Upon the ocean! Friend,
    Calm seas attend,
Soft breezes waft thee on thy way,
Safe borne to Mitylene bay!

And on that happy day I'll wreathe my head
With dill, white-flowering stock and roses red;
And from the bowl I'll quaff the Ptelian wine
And feed on roasted beans as I recline
   Beside the hearth; and I
   Full cubit-high
With curling celery will spread,
Fleabane and asphodel, my bed.

There shall I lie and, drinking at my ease,
Remember thee and press my lip to the lees,
While shepherds twain shall pipe to pleasure me,
One from Acharnae, one from Lycope;
   And Tityrus shall sing
   The sorrowing
Of hills and dirge of oaks that grow
On Himera's banks for Daphnis' woe.

How for the love of Xenea Daphnis lay
Wasting like snow that on a summer's day
Melts 'neath high Haemus, Athos, Rhodope
Or Caucasus' remotest range; and he
   Close by my side shall sing
   How once the impious king
Closed in a cedarn chest alive
The goatherd, and the busy hive

Sent to the fragrant coffer from the leas,
Bearing soft flowers for food, the blunt-faced bees,
For that the Muse had poured ambrosial wine
Upon his lips; ah, blest Comatas, thine
   To endure this happy fate,
   Incarcerate
All springtime in a cedarn tomb
Fed by the bees on honeycomb!

Would that thou hadst been living in my time
That thy inspiréd song, poet divine,
Might have delighted me, music sublime,
Rising from thy sweet lips 'neath oak or pine,
    The while thy herds I tended!'

So Lycidas sang and ended.
Then in my turn I spoke such words as these:

'Me too the Nymphs have taught, friend Lycidas,
Many a lesson, while upon the hills
My herd I tended—pastoral songs, sweet songs,
Whose melody e'en to the throne of Zeus
Rumour, maybe, has carried; but of all
This that I'll sing to honour thee is best;
Give ear then; for the Muses love thee well.

                    Simichidas sings
Myrto I love, I, poor Simichidas,
    As fondly as the goats love spring; the Loves
Accord fair omens to my suit. Alas,
    What passionate desire Aratus moves,
        His heart afire
        With love for a boy! Aristis, whose sweet lyre

Phoebus himself would hear unenviously
    By his own tripods, noble bard, full well
Knows how this love consumes him. Pan, to thee
    Who in the plain of Homole dost dwell
        I cry! Those charms
        Lay thou unsummoned in my dear friend's arms,

Or spoilt Philinus or another boy!
    Dear Pan, if thou be willing, nevermore
May boys of Arcady their squills employ

To flog thy flanks, vengeful for scanty store
    Of plenishing;
    If thou consent not, then may vermin sting

And bite thy flesh till thy nails everywhere
    Score thee; in nettles may'st thou make thy bed,
And in the cold midwinter wander bare
    On the Edonian hills uncomforted
        In the far north
        Toward Hebrus; and in summer fare thee forth

To herd thy flock beneath the Blemyan peaks
    Mid Ethiopians far, where no more flows
The Nile! But O ye Loves with rosy cheeks,
    Rosy as apples, wound me with your bows
        Philinus fair,
        Who drives my friend unpitied to despair!

Leave ye for this or Hyetis' sweet wells
    Or Byblis or steep Oecus' lofty throne,
Where golden-tresséd Aphrodite dwells!
    "Truly Philinus' charms are overblown
        Like a ripe pear!"
        So cry the women, "Art no longer fair!"

Enough, Aratus! No more sentry-go,
    Guarding his door and tramping! Other fool
With frozen limbs may hear the morn cock crow!
    Be Molon throttled in that wrestling-school!
        Let ours be peace
        And a wise crone to cause all ills to cease!'

So sang I and, still laughing pleasantly,
Lycidas handed me his stick to mark
Our brotherhood in the sweet art of song.

Then went he leftward on the road that bends
To Pyxa, while with Eucritus I turned
And fair Amyntas towards the way that leads
To Phrasidamus' farm; and, there arrived,
On couches of sweet rush we laid us down
Mid vine-leaves newly stripped, right glad to rest.
Poplars and elm-trees whispered overhead;
Near by, the sacred water from the cave
Of the Nymphs fell plashing; on the shady boughs
Dark-hued cicadas chattered ceaselessly;
Far off the tree-frog uttered his hoarse note
In the dense thicket; larks and linnets sang;
The turtle-dove made moan; about the spring
Bees flitted murmuring; fragrance everywhere
Of fruitage and rich harvest filled the air.
Pears at our feet and apples by our side
Rolled on the grass in plenty, and the boughs
Hung to the ground sloe-burdened; and the pitch
That for four years had sealed the wine-jar's head
Was loosened. Was it such a bowl as this,
Castalian Nymphs that haunt Parnassus' steep,
That aged Chiron served to Heracles
In Pholus' rocky cave? Was it such wine,
Such nectar, made the mighty Cyclops dance
Among his sheepfolds by Anapus, him
Who hurled the mountains at the Wanderer's ships?
Such nectar as ye Nymphs that harvest day
Mixed for our drinking by the altar stone
Of great Demeter of the Threshing-floor!
Now may I plant upon her heap of grain
The shovel, labour done, the while she smiles,
Corn-sheaves and poppies held in either hand!

DAPHNIS AND MENALCAS (i)

It happened on a certain day
Menalcas—so men say—
   Herding his sheep upon the steep
Met Daphnis by the way
   Tending his kine, and both were young,
   Ruddy of locks, of golden tongue,
Pipers adept were they.

And at the meeting straight spoke he,
'O Daphnis, sing with me,
   Thou guardian of the lowing kine,
   And so the choice of song be mine,
I swear I'll vanquish thee!'

Then answered Daphnis, 'Choose the song,
Menalcas, short or long,
   Shepherd of fleecy sheep, and ere
   Thou vanquish me, thou'lt yield, I swear,
Or do thy lungs a wrong!'

Menalcas Wilt thou compete then? Wilt thou set a stake?
Daphnis Aye, that I will! A stake shall back my song!
M. What shall we set to satisfy us both?
D. I'll stake a calf and do thou stake a lamb
   Big as the ewe that bore it.
M.   Nay, not so;
   Strict are my parents; every night they count
   The sheep and lambs.
D.   What then wilt stake? What prize
   Shall be the victor's?
M.   Here's a pipe I've made,

A lovely pipe, nine-reeded, joined with wax,
White wax, at top and bottom evenly.
That will I stake, but not my father's lambs.

D.   I too have such a pipe—nine reeds, white wax;
Of late I made it; still this finger's sore
Where the reed split and cut me.

M.   Who shall judge?
Who'll listen to our singing?

D.   Why, let's call
That goatherd yonder, where White-Patch the dog
Is barking round his kids.

                    Loudly the boys
Shouted; the rustic heard their call and came.
Keen were the boys to sing and he to judge.
First then Menalcas raised his tuneful voice—
For so the lot had fallen—and in turn
Sang Daphnis, answering with pastoral strain.

M.   Ye valleys and streams that from Helicon flow,
        If ever with piper's art
Menalcas hath pleased you, sweet fodder bestow
        On his lambs with a generous heart!
And if Daphnis bring heifers, then welcome and bless
His calves with an equal plenteousness!

D.   Ye fountains and meadows with herbage sweet,
        If Daphnis with voice divine
Sings songs that with Philomel's notes compete,
        Then fatten, I pray, his kine!
And welcome ye aught that Menalcas may bring
With abundance of pasture and plenishing!

M.   Where beautiful Milon plants his feet,
        The flocks bear twins and the trees

Grow tall, and the hives with honey sweet
    Are filled by the laden bees!
Let Milon be gone and the pastures are dry
And the shepherd is parched 'neath a burning sky!

D.   Where loveliest Nais is walking abroad,
      There's spring and the grass grows green;
    There udders pour richly their milky load
      The fattest of calves to wean!
    Let Nais be gone and there wither away
    The herdsman and kine in the heat of the day!

M.   Nor the riches of Croesus nor Pelops' land
      Do I crave, nor my way to wing
    More swift than the hurrying wind I demand,
      But with thee in my arms to sing
    And watch, as I sit by the sheltering rock,
    The waves of the sea and my grazing flock.

D.   Dread danger is drought to the waters; the trees
      Fear the force of the tempest; afraid
    Are birds of the snare, game of nets; ill at ease
      Is a man for the love of a maid.
    Father Zeus, not alone sick for love do I languish;
    Thou knowest, thou too, passion's fury and anguish!

So sang the boys in turn, and once again
Menalcas, singing, led the final strain:

    Spare thou my kids, O wolf,
      And spare my dams to maul!
    Do me no harm! My flock is large,
      And I who herd them small!

    Dost sleep so sound, my dog,
      Lampurus? Surely sleep

Profound befits not one who aids
   A boy to tend his sheep!

Now on the tender grass
   Shrink not, my ewes, to feed;
For ere ye weary, once again
   'Twill grow to meet your need.

Fill full your teats with milk;
   Feed on, feed on, my flock,
That some the lambs may drink and some
   With curd the crates may stock.

Then in reply sang clear-voiced Daphnis thus:

Me too from out her cave
   A close-browed maiden spied
As yesterday I drove my cows:
   'Fair, fair is he!' she cried.

No answer passed my lips,
   Nor bitter word nor gay,
But on the ground I bent my eyes
   And went my silent way.

How sweet the heifer's voice!
   How sweet her breath! To dream
How sweet in summer, idly couched
   Beside the running stream!

Acorns adorn the oak,
   Apples the apple-tree;
Cows glory in their calves, and kine
   Bring sole delight to me!

So sang the boys and thus the goatherd spake:
'Sweet, Daphnis, are thy lips and sweet thy voice;
To hear thy minstrelsy delights me more
Than to sip honey! Take thou then the pipes,
For I account thee victor in the test.
If, as I herd my goats beside thy goats,
Thou'lt be my tutor in the art of song,
Yon stump-horned goat, whose udders fill the pail
To brimming, be the guerdon for thy toil.'

As might a glad fawn leap about its dam,
So leapt the lad for pleasure and rejoiced,
Clapping his hands in triumph; as a maid
Grieves for the parting on her marriage-day,
So sat the other, sorrowing, sad at heart.
And from that day was Daphnis reckoned first
Among the herdsmen, and, while yet a boy
Of tender years, won Nais for his bride.

IDYLL IX

DAPHNIS AND MENALCAS (ii)

Sing, Daphnis, thou first, and Menalcas, a pastoral lay,
Be the calves with the cows, and the bulls with the heifers at
                                                    play;
Let them feed on the mead mid the flowers, nor afar let them
                                                    stray,
    And Daphnis here, Menalcas there,
    Sing each for me a rustic air.

                Daphnis sings
        Sweetly the calves low;
        Sweetly moos the cow;

41

Sweetly the pipes play;
Sweet the oxherd's lay;
    Sweetly sing I.
    By the cool stream I lie
On my bed softly lined;
For the rough south-western wind
    Tossed from the cliff's steep sides
My fair white heifers as they fed
    On the arbutus, and their hides
Are now my deep-piled bed.
    Tell me, what wayward child
    In love, ungoverned, wild,
Will heed his parents' chiding?
    So heed not I the rays
Of the scorching sun, abiding
    On my sweet couch these summer days.

Thus Daphnis sang to me, Menalcas thus:

Menalcas sings
Dear Mother Etna, a beautiful cave
    Is mine to dwell in mid hollow rocks;
And all men crave in dreams I have,
    Nannies and ewes; and countless flocks
Afford me fleeces to warm my bed;
And when my oak-wood fire glows red,
    Sweet honey-cakes the logs are toasting,
    Dry acorns roasting,
    What time the wintry ground
    Freezes ice-bound.
Who chooses nuts when cakes are by,
If he be toothless? So too I
    Woo not the winter cold,
    But in warm wraps my limbs enfold.

I praised their songs and clapped my hands
    And gave them each a prize;
To Daphnis a staff from my father's lands,
    Just as it grew, but of shape and size
    No craftsman would despise.
To Menalcas too a trumpet-shell
    I had plucked on the rocky shore,
And the fish had served for meat right well
    Myself and my comrades four.
And on that conch Menalcas blew
A blast of triumph, loud and true.

Hail, Muses of the country, now reveal
    The song that once I sang when with these twain
I companied; nor let me longer feel
    These pimples on my tongue, the hoarder's bane!

I sing

Cicada loves cicada, ant loves ant,
    And hawk is dear to hawk; so dear to me
    The Muse and minstrelsy.
For ever in my house may Muses grant
    Their favours! Not more sweet spring's sudden coming
    Nor sleep, nor to the humming
Bees sweet-honeyed flowers than to my ear
    The Muses' melodies; for whom they charm
    Can Circe's magic harm?
Those whom the Muses love no potions fear!

THE REAPERS

Milon   Whatever's the matter with you, my man?
You wretched Bucaeus, your swathe's not straight!
You used to drive straight, so I know you can;
And you lag in the reaping behind your mate!
You're just like a ewe that hobbles along
With a thorn in her foot behind the rest.
Then where will you be when the sun is strong,
Or sets in the evening, if that's your best?

Bucaeus You're made of granite, Milon! You can reap
Till the sun goes down; but did you never chance
To long for one that's absent?

M.   No indeed!
A labourer's business is to stick to work,
Not hanker after things outside his job.

B.   And did you never lie awake for love?

M.   No, never! And I hope I never shall!
A dog tastes leather and he'll not let go.

B.   But, Milon, I'm in love—near ten days now.

M.   You've got the cask to draw from, plain enough!
My drink's sour vinegar—not much of that!

B.   I haven't hoed the ground before my door
Since seed-time, and my love's the reason why.

M.   Which girl's your torment?

B.   Polybotas's,
She that was playing on the pipe that day
To please the reapers at Hippocion's.

M.   God's vengeance! Well, you've asked for it and got it!
A cuddling grasshopper to warm your bed!

B.   You're laughing at me; but the god of love,
Eros the careless, like the god of wealth,

Is blind! Stop bragging!

M.   Bragging? That I'm not!
Have done with reaping for a bit; strike up
Some serenade; you used to sing quite well;
And that'll add some pleasure to your work.

Bucaeus Pierian Muses, hymn with me the fair
         Maid of the flute, with slender grace endued!
All things ye touch are lovely; all decry
Thy beauty, call thee Syrian, sunburnt, spare,
And only I,
         I call thee golden, honey-hued.

Dark is the purple violet, dark as thou
         The lettered hyacinth, yet these adorn,
First of all flowers, the garland; as moon-clover
Maddens the goat, as cranes pursue the plough,
So I, thy lover,
         Follow my love, on wings of passion borne!

Ah! would I owned such wealth as men suppose
         Old Croesus owned! Then should we stand, we two,
Sculptured in gold as offerings to the Maid;
Thou with thy pipes, an apple or a rose,
And I arrayed
         In new Amyclean shoes and raiment new!

Maid of the flute, well-turned thine ankles gleam;
Thy voice enchants me, as an opium dream
The drug-bemused; I have no power to praise
The sweet beguilement of thy various ways!

Milon   Oh! What a poet, and we never knew it!
Just mark the measure, harmony and style!

45

So young! I'm blushing for my futile beard!
Now listen; these are Lityerses' lines:

Fruitful Demeter, Queen of harvest, grant
This crop be easy won, luxuriant.

Bind up the stooks, ye binders! Let none say
'Here be poor workers! What a waste of pay!'

See, when you cut your crop, the stumps look west
Or north; that way the grain is at its best.

If threshing, sleep not when the sun is high;
The grain and stalk part easier when they're dry.

But when you reap, start with the waking lark;
Rest in the heat and only stop at dark.

Carefree the frog, my lads; no slave needs he
To pour his drink; it's his ungrudgingly.

Boil up the lentils, steward—more and nicer!
Don't cut your stingy fingers, cummin-slicer!

  That's the sort of thing
  For labourers to sing
  When the sun is up and burning overhead.
  As for your tale of love,
  It's only fit to move
  Your mother of a morning in her bed!

CYCLOPS

Nor ointment, Nicias, nor salve can heal
The wounds of love; no remedy avails
Save only song; this is a gentle cure
And easeful; but how hard to attain, as thou,
Learned in physic, by the Nine beloved,
Canst testify. So Polyphemus found,
My countryman, the Cyclops, when the down
Lay fresh on lips and cheeks; maddened with love
For Galatea, counting all as nought—
Rose, apple, locks—he urged his passionate suit
With forthright frenzy; often to the fold
His flock returned untended from the fields,
While he sat wasting on the wrack-strewn shore,
Companionless, and sang from early dawn
Of Galatea, striving to assuage
The grievous hurt that Aphrodite's shaft
Had dealt his heart, deep down. So, seated there
On a high rock, eye bent upon the sea,
He sang, and knew the healing power of song.

White Galatea, milk-white nymph, agleam
   With the sheen of the unripe grape, more soft than wool,
   More playful than the calf, why dost befool
And spurn thy lover? When perchance I dream,
Thou'rt near me; when sweet slumber lifts its spell,
   Thou'rt gone, straight fleeing, as the ewe at sight
   Of the grey wolf starts up to instant flight.
'Twas on the mountain, maiden, it befell
   I loved thee first, when in those golden hours
   Thou camest with thy mother gathering flowers;
I showed the way, I saw thee, loved thee; now

My love is deathless; naught, naught carest thou!

O beauteous Galatea, well I know
   Why thou dost flee; o'er my whole forehead's space
   From ear to ear one brow deforms this face,
Stretching athwart, one long, one shaggy brow,
And one the eye beneath it, yea, and wide
   The nostril o'er my lip; yet, though absurd
   And monstrous, there's a thousand kine I herd
That give rich milk to draw and drink; beside,
   I lack no cheese either in summer time,
   Or when the leaves are falling, or when rime
Whitens the earth in winter; still my store
Burdens the cheese-racks on my cavern floor.

No Cyclops in these caverns vies with me
   In piping; ah, how oft in deepest night
   I sing of thee, my honey-sweet delight,
And of my love! Eleven fawns for thee,
All collared, and four cubs I rear! The wave
   May beat upon the shore its dark-green crest;
   Leave thou its pulsing! Come, and thou shalt rest
More sweetly sheltered in my bowery cave!
   For here are bay and slender yew and vine,
   Grapes and dark ivy; cooler far than wine
Draughts from the snows of wooded Etna; these
Be thy delights! Forswear the billowing seas!

Is it myself thou deem'st too shaggy? See,
   Here in my cave are oak-logs, here is fire
   Still red beneath the ash; be that love's pyre!
Burn thou my soul, burn that most dear to me,
My single eye! Had I some finny dower,
   Deep would I dive to thee and kiss thy hand,
   Didst thou deny thy lips, and from the land

Bring thee soft poppy, scarlet-petalled flower,
    Or snowdrop white; I cannot offer both;
    This blooms in winter, that's a summer's growth.
I'd learn to swim, if some strange ship should come,
To find what pleasures thee in thy deep home.

Come, Galatea, come thou forth! No more
    Dwell on thy home, as I no more on mine!
    Shepherd the flocks with me, with me be thine
To milk the ewes and set the cheese in store
With acid rennet. Her alone I blame,
    My mother, who hath watched me waste away,
    Grow thin and ever thinner day by day,
Yet, stony-hearted, ne'er hath breathed my name
    To plead my cause with thee! Mother, my brow
    Aches and my feet are throbbing! Suffer thou
As I am suffering, just recompense!
O Cyclops, whither flown thy crazed sense?

Far better were it didst thou plait and bind
    Cheese-crates and pluck green leaves to feed thy lambs!
    Milk thou the ewe that's nigh! Chase not the rams
That flee thy handling! It may be thou'lt find
Another Galatea, fairer still.
    Many the maids who call me in the night
    To dalliance, and I hear their laughter light
Whene'er I heed their call and serve their will.
    Doubt not, despised by sea, I still command
    The esteem of all who own my worth on land!

Thus Polyphemus sang; not gold could prove
A palliative more sure for thwarted love.

THE HEARER

Thou art come, dear boy, after so long a space—
Two nights and days; old age comes on apace,
In a single day, for those who yearn.
Sweeter than winter falls the spring;
Sweeter the apple than the sloe;
Shaggier the ewes' than the lambs' deep wool,
And more desirable the maid
Than the thrice-wedded wife;
The fawn's foot than the calf's is fleeter;
The clear-voiced nightingale sings sweeter
Than any other winged thing.
So welcome I thy glad return
More than aught else in life,
And with swift-hasting foot I go
To greet thee, as the traveller,
Scorched by the sun, seeks the oak's cool
And grateful shade.

Would that thou lovedst me as I love thee
And we were a song for all men yet to be:
'Divine these two in olden days,
One to Inspire (in Amyclean speech)
And one to Hear (in the Thessalian phrase);
In even measure each loved each—
An age of gold, when love begat like love!'
O Father Zeus, Immortals ever young,
So may our love be sung
That when, two hundred generations flown,
One brings me word to Acheron,
Whence there is no return, this I may hear:
'Thy love a theme for song shall prove,

And the true love of him thou holdest dear,
For all men, most of all for youth!'
And yet in truth
Supreme disposers are the gods above;
Their will be done!

But when I praise thee, dearest boy,
I speak no lie; for if thou painest me,
Straight dost thou heal the wound; a double joy
Beyond all measure is my joy in thee!
Skilled at the oar, ye men of Megara,
Nisaeans, happy may ye dwell,
For that ye honoured him of Attica,
The stranger Diocles, who loved so well.
Ever about his tomb,
At the first blush of spring,
The boys assembled come
To strive with kisses sweet to bring
The trophy home.
And he whose kisses sweetest are decreed
Runs to his mother, garlanded.
Happy the judge! He prays to Ganymede,
The bright-eyed boy, that on his lips be shed
That influence whereby, as the Lydian stone
Tells counterfeit from true, the sweetest kiss be known.

IDYLL XIII

HYLAS

When we were young we thought that Love
Was born our hearts alone to move,
O Nicias, and fair seemed then
Fair to us first of mortal men,

Who know not what of pain or joy
The morrow holds.
                    He loved a boy,
Amphitryon's valiant-hearted scion,
Who tamed the wild Nemean lion—
Even he loved Hylas, gracious youth
With unshorn tresses; and in truth
So loved him as a father's heart
Yearns o'er his son, and strove to impart
Learning to win the boy renown
For deathless deeds to match his own.
He would not leave him, nor when morn
Climbed to the zenith, fleetly borne
By her white steeds, nor when the heaven
Was bright at noon, nor yet at even,
When the hen-mother clapped her wings
To call her twittering fosterlings
To share her smoke-stained perch; that so
Apt to his mind the boy might grow
To heroic stature.
                    On a day
When Jason's stout-benched Argo lay
Off rich Iolcus, fitly manned
By all the noblest of the land,
Princes from every town of Greece
Chosen to seek the Golden Fleece,
Came he who countless toils had seen,
Son of Alcmene, Midea's queen,
Down to the ship, and by his side
Hylas—that Argo swift to glide
The dark-blue Clashing Rocks betwixt.
(Baffled, from then the Rocks stand fixed).

And when arose the Pleiades
And young lambs grazed on upland leas

And summer followed spring, why, then
That godlike band of valiant men
Thought on their sailing; straight they manned
The hollow ship, and fairly fanned
By a south breeze, three days they rode
To the Hellespont, and there abode
Anchored within Propontis, where
The Cian oxen draw the share
To plough broad furrows. Out on the beach
They leapt to cook their supper, each
With one fair friend; one meadow, lush
With galingale and pointed rush,
Lent its abundant store to strew
Couches for all the heroic crew.

Now Hylas golden-tressed was gone,
Bidden by steadfast Telamon
And Heracles, to seek a spring
And in his brazen pitcher bring
Water to serve the meal they shared.
So on a chance as forth he fared,
A deep-set spring he spied; the ground
Was rife with rushes all around,
Wild celery, dark celandine
And maidenhair with fronds of green
And creeping dog's-tooth grass; and lo!
Nymphs in the water far below
Were dancing, sleepless Nymphs and dread,
Sore peril to the country-bred;
Nycheia with her April glance,
Malis, Eunica led the dance.

All eagerly he scanned the pool
And reached to fill his pitcher full;
But as he reached, the love-struck band

Of dancing Nymphs clung to his hand,
Passionately tender; as some star
Shoots blazing from the heavens afar
To strike the sea, and sailors call,
'A breeze! A breeze! Make ready all!'
So Hylas fell, drawn down by love,
And the dark waters closed above.

The watery Nymphs with accents mild
Strove to console the weeping child,
Laying him on their laps; but mad
With grief to seek the dear lost lad
Forth Heracles, Amphitryon's son,
Grasping his well-tried club, was gone,
And his curved bow was by his side.
'Hylas!' and 'Hylas!' loud he cried,
'Hylas!' again; the frenzied note
Burst from the cavern of his throat.
Thrice echoing came the answering cry,
He heard it not; how nigh, how nigh
Lost Hylas! But remote and faint
Sounded deep down the boy's sad plaint.

As when the ravening lion at dawn
Hears the far cry of the mountain fawn,
And straight bounds forth to snatch the prize,
A promised meal, from where he lies,
So ranged the hero, all distraught
With yearning for the boy he sought.
O'er the untrodden thorns he hied
Raging; no track was left untried.
Reckless are lovers; heeding not
Sore toil, all Jason's quest forgot,
Through thickset brakes that stayed his tread,
O'er steeps where'er his footsteps led,

Madly he searched.

                The Argonauts,
Sails set, full-manned the oarsmen's thwarts,
Waited his coming, stayed in vain;
Fell midnight; sails were lowered again.
Cruel the wounding god who drove
The hero on; his name was Love!

'Deserter!' jeered the abandoned crew,
As on to Colchis Argo flew,
Brave ship of sixty oars, and bore
Its freight to the unwelcoming shore
Of Phasis. Last, foot-weary, came
Heracles, mocked, a name of shame;
But Hylas fair had won immortal fame!

IDYLL XIV

AESCHINAS AND THYONICHUS

Aeschinas   A very good day, my Thyonichus.
Thyonichus And a very good morning to you.
             It's long since you've favoured me.
A.   Yes, it is.
T.   And why are you looking so blue?
A.   I'm terribly worried, Thyonichus.
T.   Then that's why you're haggard and lean,
             With a straggly moustache and a barbarous
             Profusion of locks—as I've seen
             Quite lately a barefooted fellow,
             A Pythagoristic, he said,
             From Athens—complexion pale yellow.
A.   In love?
T.   With the best kind of bread!

A.   Always joking! Account for my sadness?
        She slights me, Cynisca the fair!
        I think I'm half crazy; between me and madness
        There's barely the breadth of a hair!

T.   That's just like you, always in haste,
        Impetuous, easily flurried;
        What's more, you want everything pat to your
                                            taste!

        Say, Aeschinas, why are you worried?

A.   Well here's the story; there were four of us,
        Cleunicus of the tenth, the Argive, I
        And Agis—he's the man who keeps a stud
        In Thessaly; we four were making merry
        On my estate in the country. There was roast,
        Two chickens and a piglet; and for wine
        A jar of Bibline, four years old, as fine
        In bouquet as the day the grape was pressed;
        Onions and snails to boot—a first-class spread.
        The drinking-bout was on and we agreed
        That each in turn should name his special friend
        And toast him in the neat; and so we did;
        We called the names and drank, but what d'you
                                        think?
        Cynisca, who was there, said not a word,
        Though I was present! Could I stomach that?
        Someone called out in jest, 'Struck dumb, my girl?
        'You must have seen a wolf!' She blushed so red
        You might have lit a candle at her cheeks.
        'You've got some sense!' she cried. A Wolf there is,
        Young Wolf, that Labes' son, who lives next door.
        He's tall and soft, and handsome, many think.
        So that's the boy, Cynisca's famous flame!
        I'd heard it whispered once, quite quietly,
        But paid no heed to it—stupid for my age!

Well, we were drinking deep, all four of us,
And Agis sang 'My Wolf' right through, the brute,
Some rude Thessalian ditty; all at once
Cynisca started howling like a child,
A six-year-old, crying for mother's lap!
Thyonichus, you know my hasty temper—
I boxed her ears—one, two—and off she went,
Picked up her skirts and flew! 'All right, you pest!
I'm nothing to you now!' I cried, 'Go on,
Cuddle your other darling! It's for him
You're weeping? Right! Weep apples!' Like a bird
That brings a titbit to her young in the nest
Beneath the eaves and swiftly flies again
To find another, quicker still Cynisca
Left her soft seat, flew through the porch and door,
Caring not where she went. As the old tale runs,
'The bull went off to the wood.' It's twenty days
And eight and nine, ten more, eleventh today,
Add two—that makes two months of separation.
For all she knows I've had a Thracian cut!
Now it's all 'Wolf!', an open door for 'Wolf'
Even at night! I'm nothing, bottom-most
Like the unfortunate Megarians!
I'm the mouse in the pitch-pot; where am I to find
A remedy for unrequited love?
There's Simus—he's the man who fell in love
With the brazen hussy—went to foreign parts
And came back cured; he's just about my age.
I'll go for a soldier overseas, like him;
Soldiering's not so bad, and not so good,
But much the same as any other trade.

T.   I wish you'd had your way, friend Aeschinas;
But if you're really keen to go abroad,
Go serve with Ptolemy; he'll pay you best.

57

A.	And what's he like besides?
T.	There's no one better;

Warm-hearted, patron of the arts and love,
Courteous as may be, knows his friends and knows
His unfriends better still, scatters largesse
To all and sundry, never says one nay;
That's as a king should be; but, Aeschinas,
Don't ask too much! Well, if you're really set
On joining up, and if you're brave enough
To stand your ground against a bold foe's charge,
Then off to Egypt! Imperceptibly
We all grow grey, and Time the whitener
Creeps down our cheeks. Ere age has sapped our
strength
And dried our limbs, we should be up and doing!

IDYLL XV

GORGO AND PRAXINOE

Gorgo	Are you at home, Praxinoe?
Praxinoe	At last!

Dear Gorgo, here I am. But I'm surprised
You've got here even now. A stool, Eunoa,
And find a cushion for it.

G.	Please don't bother.
P.	Do take a seat.
G.	Oh dear, Praxinoe,

I'm helpless in a crowd! That press, those chariots!
Nothing but hobnailed boots and uniforms!
I can't think how I managed to survive!
And such a journey! Every time your house
Seems further off!

P.	Well, blame my crazy man.

He's come to the end of the world and bought a hole,
It's not a house, simply to cut us off
From being neighbours—spiteful, surly brute!
That's him all over!

G.   Hush, my dear—the child!
Don't let him hear you talk like that of Dinon.
See how surprised he looks. Now, now, my pet,
Mummy's not talking about Dad, Zopyrion.

P. I do believe the child does understand!

G. Nice Daddy!

P.   Daddy! What d'you think he did
Only the other day? I sent him shopping
For soap and rouge, and back he came with salt!
The gawky creature!

G.   Just like Diocleidas;
The idiot doesn't know what money means.
He bought five fleeces yesterday—dog's hair,
Wool mangy as old wallets, foul with dirt,
All extra work for me—and spent seven drachmas!
Enough of that; on with your dress and scarf;
Let's go and see the Adonis in the palace
Of rich king Ptolemy; I hear the queen's
Got up a splendid show.

P.   All's grand for the grand!

G. What sights you'll see and what you'll have to tell
Your friends who've never been there! Let's be off;
It's time to go.

P.   Perpetual holiday
For the work-shy! Pick that spinning up, Eunoa,
And just you dare to drop it there again!
Cats love soft wool to sleep on! Stir your stumps!
Quick with the water! Now she brings me soap
When I want water first! Still, give it me—
Not all that soap, you thief! Now water! Fool!
My dress—you're drenching it! Enough! I've washed

As well as may be. Where's the key of the chest?
Come, bring it here.
G.   That dress, Praxinoe,
With its flowing folds, becomes you splendidly.
What did you pay for the material?
P.   Oh, don't remind me Gorgo! What a price!
More than two minas! And the work I've done—
My very heart and soul's been spent on it!
G.   Well, it's turned out first-class; that you can say.
P.   Bring me my scarf and hat; put them on straight.
No, I shan't take you, Baby; Horsy bites!
Bugaboo! You're not going to come home lame,
However much you cry! Come on, let's go.
Phrygia, take the child and play with him;
Call the dog in and lock the street-door after us.

Ye gods, the crowd! It's like a plague of ants,
Numberless! How on earth can we get through?
Well, anyhow things are much better now,
Ptolemy, since your father joined the gods.
No villain creeps up in the Egyptian style
And slogs you as you walk along the street,
The trick those mischievous scoundrels used to play,
Nothing to choose between them, cursed crew
With their rascalities! Dear Gorgo, look!
Here come the royal chargers! What's to do?
Don't tread on me, good fellow! See, that bay
Reared up—how wild he is! Look out, Eunoa,
You careless girl! He'll be the death of the man
That's leading him! How glad I am I left
The baby safe at home!
G.   Cheer up, Praxinoe,
They've passed us now and gone on to their post.
P.   Yes, now I've quite recovered; horse and snake
Have always been my nightmares from a child.

60

Let's hurry; what a mob comes flooding on!
G.   From the palace, mother?
Old Woman   Yes, my children, yes.
G.   Then there's a chance of getting in?
O.W.   The Greeks
Got into Troy by trying, pretty maids!
All's done by trying.
G.   Off she goes, the ancient,
Delivered of her oracle!
P.   There's nothing
Women don't know—even how Zeus wed Hera!
G.   See all those people milling round the gates,
Praxinoe.
P.   Stupendous! Hold my hand,
Gorgo, and you, Eunoa, take her maid's.
Keep close to us, Eunoa. Oh, dear dear!
Gorgo, my scarf is torn in two already!
By Zeus, good fellow, as you hope for heaven,
Do mind my scarf!
First Stranger   I'm not responsible,
But still I'll do my best.
P.   It *is* a mob,
Like jostling pigs.
F. S.   Don't panic, dame; all's well.
P.   May all be well with you now and for ever,
Our kind protector! What a nice good man!
Eunoa's being crushed! You silly girl,
Force your way through the crowd! Good! 'All
                            inside!'
As the bridegroom said when he shut the door on the
                             bride.

G.   What lovely tapestries! What delicate work!
You'd say that gods might hang them! Come,
                         Praxinoe,
Look at them first!

P.   Goddess of handicraft!
        What weavers can have woven them? Such lines,
        So true! What artists could design those forms?
        How naturally they stand and seem to move
        As if alive, not woven! Man's a marvel!
        And there's Adonis in his silver chair;
        How wonderful he looks, with the first down
        Soft on his cheeks—Adonis most beloved,
        Even in death beloved!
Second Stranger   Do stop that chattering!
        You wretched turtles—on and on—a, a!
        Broad Dorian, it'll be the death of me!
P.   Ho! Where's this fellow from? What's it to you
        If we do chatter? Order about your slaves!
        We're Syracusans, and I'd have you know
        We're sprung from Corinth, like Bellerophon!
        Peloponesian's what we talk; I fancy
        Dorians may talk Dorian? O Persephone,
        One lord's enough for us! A fig for you!
        Don't waste your time levelling empty pots!
G.   Quiet, Praxinoe, she's going to sing
        The Adonis-hymn—the Argive woman's daughter,
        That clever singer who won the prize last year
        For the lament; she'll be worth listening to,
        I'm sure of that; she's just about to start.

The Song
    O Cyprian Lady, who hauntest the shady
        Groves of Idalium and Golgi the olden,
    On Eryx thou rovest, the steep that thou lovest,
        Most fair Aphrodite, whose playthings are golden!
    See how the Hours, the dear Hours, softly going,
        Slow-footed Hours, at the turn of the year
    Have brought thee from Acheron's stream ever-flowing
        Thy lover Adonis! To mortals how dear

Their coming, for ever some bounty bestowing!

O Lady of Cyprus, Dione's fair daughter,
   Whose gift of ambrosia—so runs the story—
Shed blessing on queen Berenice and brought her
   A place with the gods in their infinite glory!
O Lady of temples and names without ending,
   For thee queen Arsinoe, peerlessly fair,
Bestows on Adonis with lovingest tending
   All fruits in their season that orchards may bear,
And gardens from baskets of silver depending.

There to please him are perfumes from Syrian bowers
   In vials of gold; bread that many a maiden
Has kneaded, rich cakes of sweet honey and flowers,
   White meal and smooth oil, beast and bird; anise-laden
Green arbours, and over them little Loves flying
   That seem like young nightingales flitting from spray
To spray of the tree, fledgling wings newly trying.
   O well may Miletus and Samian say
'Ours, ours on the couch where Adonis is lying

'Are the crimson-hued coverlets, softer than dreaming!'
   White ivory eagles, their wings lightly laden
With Ganymede's form, gold and ebony gleaming
   Enchased on the couch where the Cyprian maiden
Lies clasped in Adonis' bright arms, and embraces
   Her lover in hers; and his kisses are smooth;
He is young and the twentieth year scarcely traces
   The light golden down on the lips of his youth.
Farewell, Aphrodite the lover! Our praises

Shall rise at the dawning, with dew on the blossoms;
   We carry him out to the waves, broken-hearted,
And loosing our tresses and baring our bosoms
   Our threnody raise for a lover departed!

Thine, dear Adonis, only thine
The gift, of heroes half-divine,
To visit earth and, springtime gone,
To tread the shores of Acheron.
Not Agamemnon knows this path
To earth, nor Aias, swift to wrath,
Nor yet the Lapiths nor the sons
Of earliest man, Deucalions,
Nor Hector, son of Hecabe,
First-born, nor yet Pelopidae
Nor Argive lords, nor Patrocles
Nor Pyrrhus back from Troy; for these
Return not. Thy return, most dear,
We look for in the circling year
And pray thy grace! How happy thou
Hast found us in thy coming now!
Again, Adonis, come to bless
Thy servants and perfect their happiness!

Gorgo   How truly marvellous that woman is,
Praxinoe! Such learning, lucky girl!
Luckier still to have that lovely voice!
Still, time for home! Diocleidas hasn't dined,
And when he's hungry, better keep well clear!
The man's all vinegar! Farewell! Returning,
Dearest Adonis, find us faring well.

IDYLL XVI

HIERO

To bard and heaven-born Muse it doth belong
Ever to praise the immortal gods in song
And the brave deeds of heroes; but the Muse

64

Must hymn her kin; she is the child of Zeus.
We mortals here below of mortals sing.
Who now receives with lavish welcoming
Our Graces? Who of all beneath the sun
Denies not guerdon when the song is done?
None! Home they travel barefoot and complain,
Upbraiding, of a toil endured in vain;
Shamefast, head bowed upon cold knees, they rest
There at the bottom of the empty chest,
Where they are wont to hide when thus returned
Bootless, disconsolate, due meed unearned.
Where now the patron? Who will grant the bard
Who sings his praise the merited reward?
I know not! Men in these degenerate days
No more, as once, compete to win high praise
For generous deeds; they are the slaves of gain
And, clasping tight their money-bags, would fain
Hunt for a bargain, nor one silver piece,
Rubbed clean of tarnish, liberally release.
Straight say they, 'Charity begins at home!
Myself would keep whatever luck may come!'
Or, 'Heaven rewards the bard!' or, 'Homer's lays
Suffice; what need of other songs? I praise
As best the bard whose minstrelsy is free!'
Good sirs, what profit lies in miserly
Hoards of uncounted gold? The wise deny
All blessing to such wealth! To satisfy
One's own desires and to reward the art
Of some poor poet, with ungrudging heart
Cherish one's kin and others, day by day
Offer due sacrifice to God, never to play
The churlish host but grace the stranger guest
With all one's table offers of the best
And speed him when departing—this indeed
Is truest wealth; but most of all just meed

To grant the poet, and to wreathe with bay
The inspired interpreter; then will men say,
When on the sunless shore of Acheron
Unseen thou hidest, bloodless shade and wan,
'This was a noble patron!' Not unsung
Like some poor horny-handed toiler, flung
Into a tomb dishonoured shalt thou fall.

Many the serfs in king Aleuas' hall
And king Antiochus's court who drew
Measured provision for their monthly due;
Many the calves were driven from the lea
With hornéd kine, herds of the Scopadae,
Bellowing to the stalls; many the choicely bred
Flocks on the plain of Crannon, pasture-fed,
Wealth of the kindly Creons; but afloat,
Sweet spirits, on grim Charon's broad-beamed boat,
What joy in these had they? Among the dead,
Luckless, forlorn and unrememberéd,
All that vast wealth forsaken, ages long
Would they have lain, had not the inspired song
Of the Cean bard, tuned to the many strings
Of the sweet zither, brought them life as kings
Famed for all time; and each swift-footed steed,
Crowned in the sacred games, won glorious meed.
Great Lycian chiefs and Cycnus maiden-white
And Priam's long-haired sons had vanished quite
Into oblivion, had bards not told
In song the warriors' battle-cries of old;
Nor had Odysseus won undying fame,
Who roamed ten years from land to land and came
Living to utmost Hades, wise to save
His comrades from the baleful Cyclops' cave;
Nor yet Eumaeus, keeper of the swine,
Nor he, that herdsman busied with the kine,

Philoetius, nor Laertes great of heart,
Had not the Ionian minstrel lent his art.

Fair fame is theirs whose deeds the Muse hath graced;
When men are dead, their wealth the living waste.
Less toil to count the waves upon the strand,
Hurled by the wind and blue-grey sea to land,
Or in clear water cleanse a mud-baked brick,
Than to persuade a miser, maimed and sick
With avarice! Farewell to such as he!
Rich may the treasure in his coffers be,
Nor may he cease to covet more! Renown
And friendship would I choose, nor rather own
Great store of mules and horses; and my quest
Is for some mortal whom as honoured guest
I may approach, companioned by the Muse.
Ill fares the minstrel whom the child of Zeus,
The mighty counsellor, will not inspire
With friendly aid! Not yet the heavens tire
Revolving months and years in fixed array;
Oft shall their steeds roll on the wheel of day;
Then shall that man appear, the man who needs
My minstrel skill, when he hath wrought such deeds
As great Achilles or, where Ilus fought
And fell on Simois' plain, dread Aias wrought.
Already where the setting sun is red,
Tremble Phoenicians of the coast for dread,
While men of Syracuse grip spear and wield
On ready arm equipped the wicker shield;
And Hiero in their midst mail-clad, arrayed
Like some old hero, helmed beneath the shade
Of the horsehair plume. O Zeus, we pray to thee,
Lord of renown, and thee, Persephone,
Who with thy mother reignest o'er the wide
City of Ephyraea, set beside

The waters of Lysimeleia's marsh,
Lady Athene too, we pray that harsh
Necessity may drive our enemies
Out from this isle over the western seas—
Few may they be—bearing dread news of bane
To wife and child—husband and father slain!
Grant ye that cities ravished by our foes
May see once more their erstwhile lords repose
In settled peace; that these may till the fields
Now fertile, while the herb each pasture yields
May fatten myriad sheep upon the plain
Bleating, and cattle, gathering once again
In twilight to their byres, while in the trees
Cicadas watch with ceaseless melodies
The sun-scorched shepherds; spiders spin their frail
Delicate webs o'er spears and coats of mail!
No more the war-cry sound! Let minstrels raise
To Hiero's name triumphant songs of praise
Across the Scythian sea to Babylon,
Walled by Semiramis to hold her throne!
One bard am I, and many more there be
The Muses love; may all unite with me
To hymn Sicilian Arethusa's fame,
To extol her warriors and exalt the name
Of spearman Hiero! Graces, goddesses
Worshipped long since by Minyan Eteocles,
O ye that love Orchomenus, the bane
Of ancient Thebes, unsummoned I remain
Here in my home; but whoso craves my skill
I hear his call, and with a ready will
Obey it; and the Muses shall inspire
My coming. What that mortal can desire
Falls to his lot that lacks the Muses' grace?
Ever be mine to share their dwelling-place!

ODE TO PTOLEMY

With Zeus let us begin and, when we sing,
Zeus, noblest of immortals, shall be found
At our song's close, O Muses; but of men
Let Ptolemy be hymned among the first
And last and in the midst, most excellent.
Heroes of old, children of demigods,
Wrought mighty deeds and found to sing their praise
Masters of poesy; but I, well skilled
To frame fair odes, must honour Ptolemy.
Even to gods are songs the guerdon paid.

On Ida's forest slopes the woodman doubts
Where first to wield his axe, so dense the trees;
What first am I to hymn of all the gifts
Wherewith the gods have graced the best of kings?

How great was Ptolemy, sprung from the great,
To plan such exploits as none other planned
And to accomplish them! Him Father Zeus
Raised to like honour with the blessed gods
And set for him in heaven a golden throne.
There by his side seated in friendly wise
Rests Alexander deified, the bane
Of Persia, on his head a diadem
Of many hues; and near them stands the throne,
Wrought of hard adamant, where Heracles
The Centaur-slayer keeps high festival
With the immortals; greatly he delights
In his sons' sons, who grow not old but rank,
His offspring, with the gods by grace of Zeus.
For both may trace, through Heracles' great son,

Their line to Heracles; so when, his fill
Of fragrant nectar quaffed, he leaves the feast
To seek his dear wife's chamber, to the one
He hands the bow and, slung beneath his arm,
The quiver, and the iron club embossed
To the other; thus accoutred they escort
To where white-ankled Hebe dwells, a bower
Ambrosial, the bearded son of Zeus.

And Berenice, born to bless her sire,
Wisest of women, far-renowned! On her
Dione's glorious daughter, Cyprus' queen,
Laid her soft hands, touching her fragrant breast,
Whence comes it, so men say, that never yet
Has wife so charmed her lord as she her spouse,
Whose love in fuller measure she returned.

So, loving to the bed of one who loves,
Might a man come, and with a cheerful heart
Trust to his sons his house and all it holds.
The unloving wife seeks happiness abroad;
Children she bears with ease unlike their sire.

O Aphrodite, fairest of the fair,
O Queen of Heaven, thy care was she; 'twas thou
Who, ere the mournful shore of Acheron
Was reached and beauteous Berenice stepped
On to the dark-prowed ferry of the dead,
Rowed by grim Charon, snatched her from death's power
And set her in thy shrine to share with thee
The honours paid thee; soft the loves she breathes
Into all hearts; by her consoling aid
The yearning lover finds his cares allayed.

Thou, Argive lady of dark brow, didst bear

To Caledonian Tydeus Diomede
The slaughterer; deep-bosomed Thetis bore
To Peleus, son of Aeacus, a son,
Spearman Achilles, like his sire; e'en so
To warrior Ptolemy thy mother bore,
Famed Berenice, warrior Ptolemy.
Thee from thy mother, as her fosterling,
Cos took and cherished, when the light of day
Broke on thine opening eyes, a babe newborn.

For there the daughter of Antigone,
Burdened with birth-pangs, called on her whose aid
Lightens the pains of travail, Eileithuia.
She by her side in kindly tendance stood
And eased the pain in all her limbs; forthwith
Was born a child, like to his sire, beloved.
And when she saw him, Cos cried out for joy,
Clasping the babe in loving hands, and said,
'Blest be thy birth, dear boy! As Phoebus once
Exalted Delos, crowned with the dark blue sea,
So honour me! As he with equal love
Cherished Rhenoea, stablish Triops' hill,
Granting like favour to the Dorian isles,
My neighbours!' Thus she spake, and from the clouds
Thrice shrieked a mighty eagle, bird of fate,
A sign from Zeus; for Zeus, old Cronos' son,
Cares for all honoured kings, but most he cares
For one he loves newborn; great wealth is his,
Many the lands he rules, many the seas.

A myriad lands, a myriad tribes of men,
Prospered by heaven-sent showers, bear ripened crops;
But none so rich as bear the Egyptian plains,
When the full-flooding Nile breaks up the clods
And soaks the soil; nor any land can count

So many towns, so many husbandmen.
Three hundred are her cities, and again
Three thousand, thrice ten thousand, and twice three
And three times nine therewith; and of all these
Lord Ptolemy is king; his rule extends
O'er Syria, Arabia, Libya
And the black hordes of Ethiopia;
Pamphylia bows before him; Lycians
And battle-loving Carians own his sway;
The island kingdoms of the Cyclades
Yield to his lordship; for the noblest ships
That sail the sea are his; yea, sea and land
And turbulent river honour him as king;
And round him gather horse and foot, a host
Shield-bearing, armoured all in glittering bronze.
Heavier his treasure in the scale than all
The wealth of other monarchs; day by day
Flows from all countries to his rich domains
Abundance, and his subjects ply their trades
In peace; no land-based enemy dare cross
The infested Nile to raise the battle-cry
In foreign hamlets; never foe bounds armed
From his swift ship to raid upon the shore
The herds of Egypt; for there sits enthroned
In those broad plains a king skilled with the spear,
Ptolemy golden-haired; his care to hold
All he is heir to, and himself extend
This heritage; such is the task of kings.

Heaped in his palaces lie piles of gold
Like the rich stores of still laborious ants,
Yet lie they not unused; gifts he bestows
On the magnificent temples of the gods,
First-fruits and much beside; on mighty kings,
On cities and brave comrades liberal gifts.

When in the holy Dionysiac games
Some singer, skilled to raise melodious song,
Merits a prize, 'tis his, and all the bards,
Muses' interpreters, extol the king
For his munificence. What nobler end
Can one blessed with prosperity pursue
Than to win deathless glory among men?
Glory abides, even for Atreus' house,
While all the wealth they gathered, ravaging
Priam's great halls, lost in oblivion
Lies in deep darkness, whence is no return.

He only of all men now dead and those
Whose footprints, moulded by the beaten dust
Still fresh, survive, hath stablished fragrant shrines
For his dear parents; there by filial hands
Gleaming in gold and ivory, dedicate
They stand as saviours of the sons of earth.
And on the altars, as the months revolve,
Reddened with pious sacrifice, there burn
Thighs of fat oxen; these the offerings
He makes, and by his side his glorious queen,
Than whom no wife more faithful in his halls
Clasps in her arms a spouse, with all her heart
Loving her husband-brother. Thus were joined
In holy union the immortal gods,
Whom Rhea bore monarchs of heaven; so too
Iris, still maiden, strews with perfumed hands
One couch for Zeus and Hera's bridal bed.

Farewell, King Ptolemy! Thy name I praise;
Thy rank is with the demigods; my song
Men shall approve hereafter, so I deem;
But for true worth, O king, pray thou to Zeus!

BRIDAL SONG TO HELEN

Twelve were the maidens, fairest of the fair,
Blossoms of hyacinth twined in their hair,
Fair flowers of Sparta who, conjoined as one,
Prepared the dance for Atreus' younger son,
Golden-haired Menelaus, at the hall.
To the new-painted bower, forgetting all
But his loved Helen, now his wedded bride,
Tyndareus' child, he led her; there beside
The palace door in unison they sang,
Dancing, and with their song the whole house rang.

Sleeping so early, dear bridegroom?
    Art heavy with passion for sleep?
Fuddled thy head that thou seekest thy bed
    After potions too deep?
Wert thou so eager for slumber,
    Should'st lay thee apart from thy bride,
Leaving the maid till the dawn while she played
    With her friends by her dear mother's side.
There's tomorrow and many a morrow to come
For the joy of thy bride in the bridal home.

Happy wert thou when thou camest
    To challenge the lords in their pride,
Of all heroes alone Heaven's monarch to own
    As sire of thy bride!
Surely some omen had blessed thee
    To win Heaven's child past compare,
Most peerless on earth, and the child of her birth
    Shall be wondrous as she and as fair.
Twelve score are we maidens, a virginal band;
Anointed we race on Eurotas' strand.

We are all of an age with thy lover
    But none can be matched with her grace.
Fair, Lady Night, is the rising light
    On Dawn's bright face;
Bright is the coming of springtime
    When winter is over and gone;
So with radiance rare in our company fair
    Lovely Helen the golden shone;
As tall as the cypress that stands on the mead,
As swift as the coursing Thessalian steed.

Winding the yarn from her basket,
    Shuttling the many-hued thread,
And severing deftly the close-pressed weft
    From the tall loom's head—
What can compare with her weaving?
    And who so adept with the lyre,
Sweet paeans to raise of melodious praise,
    As the queen with the eyes of desire?
Broad-bosomed Athene she hymns and she sings
Of Artemis, touching the trembling strings.

Fair maiden, no more our companion,
    Thou tendest the house of thy lord;
But tomorrow we'll speed to the blossoming mead
    With a single accord
To gather thee sweet-scented garlands
    And think on thy beauty as dear
As the breast of the dam to the tenderest lamb,
    And the low-growing lotus-leaves bear
To the shade of a plane, while the flask lets drip
Smooth oil on the sward from its silver lip.

And on the plane's bark shall be written
    In Dorian tongue clear to see

For all who pass by: 'Give me honour, for I
    Am Helen's tree.'
Fare thee well, O thou bride, and, O bridegroom,
    Farewell, prince of loftiest line!
May Leto this night bless the conjugal rite
    And may Aphrodite divine
Inspire mutual love, and high Heaven attend
Sire and son with prosperity unto life's end!

    Sleep, breathing love and yearning,
    Each into other's breast:
    And when dawn's new light
    Scatters the night,
    Forget not to rise from rest.
    In the early morning returning
    When the first bright-feathered bird
    Raises his strain,
    We shall come and again
    Our bridal song be heard.

    Hymen, O Hymenaeus!
    Joy, joy be thy glad refrain!

IDYLL XIX

THE HONEY THIEF

Love, the little robber he,
    Was stealing honey from the hive
When out there flew a sudden bee
    And stung his hand with angry dive.
Oh, how he stamped and danced and blew
    His finger-tips to ease the sting,
And straight to Aphrodite flew

Complaining, 'Such a little thing
To deal such hurt!' His mother smiled
And thus consoled her weeping boy:
'Complainest thou, beloved child?
Small bees can cause a great annoy;
Thou too art small; thy wounding dart
Can pierce full deep a lover's heart!'

IDYLL XX

THE NEATHERD

When her lips I would have won,
Eunica mocked me, cried, 'Begone!'
Laughed and spoke a taunting word,
'Kiss me, would you? Vulgar herd!
Gentle lips I've learnt to prize;
Bumpkin kisses I despise!
Not for you this lovely mouth,
Even dreaming! Talk uncouth,
Scabrous lips and horseplay rude,
Filthy fingers, glances lewd!
How you stink! Away!' with that
Thrice into her breast she spat
Lest I foul her; up and down
Scanned me o'er with angry frown;
Pursing lips of proud disdain
Played the lady, and again
Mocked me, insolently vain.

Straight into a rage I flew;
Like a rosebud washed with dew
Crimsoned at the wanton smart.
Off she went; and in my heart

I resent that such as she,
Harlot vile, should jeer at me,
Pretty fellow though I be.

Tell me, shepherds, tell me true,
Am I fair or foul to view?
Have I suffered sudden change?
Once my beauty, sweet and strange,
Clothed, as ivy clothes a tree,
Chin with beard; like celery
Curled about my temples tight
Locks luxuriant; and white
Gleamed my forehead o'er my brow
Dark as night; my eyes aglow,
Brighter than Athene's eyes,
Grey-eyed goddess; melodies
Sweet as honey from the comb
Flowed from lips, soft music's home.
Whether reed or pipe I use,
Flute or syrinx, sweet my muse;
On the hills the women call
Me fair and kiss me, one and all!
Shall this city-slut deny
Kisses thus and pass me by,
Quick to avert a scornful eye?

Neatherd I; but knows she not
Cypris once, all pride forgot,
Mad with love for such as I,
Tended kine upon the high
Phrygian hills, and in the grove
Loved Adonis, mourned her love?
And Endymion? Who was he?
Simple hind of low degree;
Yet Selene loved him well,

78

Sailing through the Latmian dell
Down from heaven to share delight
With her darling night by night.
Rhea, thou mournest for thy herd;
Zeus, in guise a wandering bird,
Plucked from earth a neatherd youth;
But Eunica—she, forsooth,
Mightier than the Cyprian's might,
Brighter than Selene bright,
Scorning Rhea, denied, unkind,
Kisses to the humble hind!

Grant, O Cyprian maid, she prove
Lone in unrequited love!
In the town and on the height
Sleep abandoned through the night!

IDYLL XXI

THE FISHERMEN

It is poverty only that fosters the crafts, Diophantus;
    She's the mistress of toil; for, beset by anxieties deep,
Scarce slumbers the labouring man, and by chance if he slumber
    A moment or two, sudden care will arouse him from sleep.

It chanced that two old fishermen
Lay in their hut of plaited boughs;
Dried seaweed was their couch, their backs
Resting against the leafy wall.
Hard by, the labour of their hands
Strewn all about them—baskets, rods,
Hooks, lines and weed-entangled lures,
Traps, pots of woven rush, oars, ropes,
Propped on its stays an aged boat,

Clothes, caps and matting for the head—
These their possessions, this their wealth.
No key, no door, no guardian dog;
What need of these? Sheer poverty
Their sole protector; not a soul
Dwelt near them; by their cabin walls
Confining ocean lapped the shore.
Not yet Selene's chariot
Had climbed high heaven when anxious thought
Of the day's toil aroused the twain.
Clearing their eyes of sleep, they turned
From inner thought to mutual speech.

Asphalion They lied, my friend, who said the summer night
    Grows shorter when the day is long;
      I've dreamt a thousand dreams, and yet the light
    Of dawn delays; the night is young.

Companion Why blame fair summer, friend Asphalion?
    'Tis not the season's wanton wrong;
    Care scatters dreaming, bids sweet sleep begone
    And makes the shortest night seem long.

    A. Hast skill to interpret dreams? My dreams are rare;
    I'll have thee share my fantasies.

    C. We share our fish; 'twere well we friends should share
    Your visions; I've the wit to guess;
    Wit is the best interpreter; till day
    We've leisure, sleepless by the sea;
    Ass in the thicket, Hestia's flame, men say
    Sleep not; so on our leaves lie we.

    A. Weary with fishing, ere the sun declined,
    I slept, nor had I supped too well;

Remember, friend, 'twas early when we dined,
   Sparingly too; as it befell,
I dreamed I perched upon a rock to wait,
   Dangling my rod, till I should catch
Some prey unwary with my tempting bait.
   Nibbled a fish; with swift dispatch
I hooked him and he bled; (you know how wish
   Governs our sleep; the coursing hound
Dreams of the elusive quarry, I of fish);
   Bent was my rod as round and round
He struggled lashing; then to full incline
   I reached; how raise that monstrous one
On my weak rod? I pricked him, slacked my line
   And tightened when he would not run.
At last I won the struggle, brought to land
   A golden fish—scales, all, of gold;
But when I saw it, sudden dread unmanned
   My limbs, lest haply overbold
I'd snatched some favourite from Poseidon's lair
   Or sea-green Amphitrite's store;
Gently I freed him, lest the hook should tear
   Gold from his mouth, and straitly swore
Never again to tempt the treacherous sea
   But lord it with my gold on land;
With that I awoke; now, comrade, counsel me;
   I tremble at my vow's demand!

C. Fear not; you vowed no vow, nor did you take
      The golden fish you fancied; lies,
   All lies your dream! I counsel you, awake,
      Not sleeping, seek such monstrous prize;
   Then is there hope your visions may be true;
      'Twere well abandon fantasies!
   Not golden dreams, but fleshly fish pursue;
      The dreamer starves, the dreamer dies!

THE DIOSCURI

Twin sons of Leda and of Zeus we hymn,
Who bears the aegis,—Polydeuces grim
To battle with the fists, the leathern thong
Bound to the palm, and Castor; twice our song,
Yea thrice, shall rise to celebrate the twain
Whom Thestius' daughter bore on Sparta's plain.
Mortals ye succour in their hour of need,
Calm on the field of blood the panicked steed
And guard from peril ships, in heaven's despite
Defying tempests and the savage might
Of turbulent waves; towering the billows ride,
Astern, ahead, to breach on either side
The timbers; down into the hold they cast
Their spumy waters; dangling from the mast
Hang shattered spar, torn sheet and tangled sail;
Then with the night strike iron rods of hail
And stormy blasts the roaring seas confuse.
Yet from the depths the ships and desperate crews
That looked on death ye rescue, and the deep
Lies smooth, the winds are stilled, the billows sleep;
Scatter the clouds and in the heaven appears
Once more the heartening vision of the Bears;
'Twixt the two Asses, dimly glimmering,
Behold the Crib, to speed fair voyaging.

Beloved Twins, men's succour, athletes strong,
Citharists, horsemen, minstrels skilled in song,
Which first to celebrate? I tune my lays
To both, but Polydeuces first I praise.

Now had the Argo fled the Clashing Rocks

And braved the snowy Pontus' fearful jaws,
Bearing her precious freight of godlike men,
So coming to the Bebryces; forthwith
From either thwart of Jason's ship there stepped
That company of heroes down to the shore,
Landing upon the wide and windless beach.
There strewed they beds and twirled in either hand
The fire-sticks; but together strayed apart,
Far from their friends, Castor, lord of swift steeds,
And sun-bronzed Polydeuces, from the hill
Viewing the varied scenes of the wild woods.
Under a smooth-faced rock they spied a spring
Where lucent water brimmed perennially;
Crystalline, silver, gleaming in its depths
Glittered the pebbles, and upon its banks
Pines stood erect and tufted cypresses,
Poplars and planes; there grew sweet-scented flowers,
A welcome harvest for the shaggy bees,
All flowers that clothe the leas in the last of spring.
Seated hard by, a monster basked in the sun;
Dread sight was he—ears crushed by iron fists,
Broad back and giant chest a steel-hard mass
Of solid flesh, like some huge statue forged
Of metal; out below the shoulders stood
Stout muscles in his arms, rounded like rocks
Whirled in some winter stream and polished smooth
In its strong eddies; from his back and neck
Hung, fastened by the paws, a lion's hide.
Him Polydeuces undefeated hailed:

Polydeuces
　　　　Good-day, whoe'er thou art! Who own this land?
Amycus　Good-day? How good, with strangers trespassing?
　P.　　Fear not! No villains we nor yet our sires.
　A.　　I know no fear; thou need'st not teach me that!

83

P.	A savage, art thou—ever rude and proud?
A.	I'm what thou see'st—at least, no trespasser.
P.	Trespass on us; we'll speed thee home with gifts.
A.	Give me no gifts! Thou'lt get no gifts from me!
P.	Not even leave to drink, sir, of this spring?
A.	Thou'lt know that when thy lips are parched with thirst!
P.	How then persuade thee? Silver, say, or what?
A.	Up with thy fists and fight me man to man!
P.	Boxing? or all-in fighting, legs and eyes?
A.	Plain fists, and do thy level best to win.
P.	Who art thou, then, to meet my thong-bound fists?
A.	He whom thou see'st—no milksop—Boxer named.
P.	What prize for the victor in our boxing-match?
A.	Thine, if thou win'st, am I; or else, thou mine.
P.	Thus scarlet-crested cocks decide their brawls.
A.	Gamecocks or lions, those the stakes we lay!

So challenged Amycus and blew a blast
On a hollow conch; in the shade of the plane-trees fast
Gathered the long-haired Bebryces; there too,
Summoned by Castor, sped the heroic crew.

Now made they firm their fists with leathern straps
And wound about their arms long thongs; so moved
With murderous zeal between the watching hosts.
Eagerly strove they which should take his stand
Unblinded by the sun; with skilful step
Brave Polydeuces foiled his monstrous foe
And won his place; full on the giant's front
Fell the disabling rays; flailing his fists,
Wrathful the foe advanced; but at the assault
Straight Polydeuces smote his chin; enraged,
Caution and skill forgot, lowering his head,
He dashed to the attack; loud cheered the host
Of Bebryces; the heroes on their part

Cried 'Courage!' to the son of Tyndareus,
Fearing lest, like the giant Tityus,
So strait the space they fought in, he should crush
Their champion; but the son of Zeus stepped in,
Now here, now there, with this hand and with that,
Slashing the skin, and stayed from the onward rush
His over-confident foe, Poseidon's son.
So stood the giant, staggered by the blows,
Spitting red blood, and all the heroes cheered
To see his mouth and jaw-bones battered sore,
His swollen face, his narrowed eyes. The prince
Then threatened, feinting in pretence to strike,
And when he marked the monster all confused,
Drove hard upon his forehead, flayed the brow
To the bone. Thus stricken Amycus supine
Lay stretched upon the blossoming mead. Once more
He rose, and ever fiercer grew the fight
As, raining blows with their stout thongs, each sought
To slay the other; but the giant chief
Smote only on the shoulders and broad breast
Of his opponent, while with pounding blows
Unconquerable Polydeuces struck
The enemy's face and smashed it to a pulp.
Sweating, Amycus' flesh collapsed; from great
He shrank to small; as grimmer grew the toil,
The other's limbs waxed stronger, brighter-hued.

How then did Polydeuces, son of Zeus,
Vanquish that glutton? Tell me thou, O Muse;
For this thou knowest; I, interpreting
Thy will to others, as it please thee, sing.

Amycus, then, set on some deed of might,
With his left hand grasped Polydeuces' left;
Slantwise inclining from his guarding arm,

Came in on the right to crash his solid fist
Up from the flank; had he not missed his mark,
Hard would have fared the prince of Amyclae.
But Polydeuces swerved, and with the strength
Of his right shoulder aiding smote the foe
On the left temple with relentless fist.
Fast from the yawning wound flowed dark red blood.
Next, with the left he struck the monster's mouth,
Rattling the serried teeth; blow after blow
He rained upon the face till either cheek
Was smashed, and Amycus bewildered fell
Prostrate upon the ground; both hands upraised,
Near dead, he owned defeat. Victorious thou,
O boxer Polydeuces, spared'st to slay
The fallen foe; but at thy hest he swore
A binding oath that never strangers more
Would meet with purposed harm; to witness it
Called on his sire, Poseidon, from the sea.

Thee have I hymned, O Prince; thee too my muse
Shall celebrate, O son of Tyndareus,
Castor, lord of swift steeds, spearman renowned,
Castor, thy breast in brazen corslet bound!

Castor and Polydeuces, sons of Zeus,
Had rapt perforce and borne away two maids,
Leucippus' daughters; but Aphareus' sons,
Lynceus and stalwart Idas, bridegrooms both
Plighted to wed them, followed vengefully
In hot pursuit; nigh to Aphareus' tomb
All leapt in the instant from their chariots
With hollow shields and spears; but Lynceus cried
With a loud voice from the shadow of his helm,
'Good sirs, why seek ye battle, arrogant
To seize the brides of others? Why thus flash

These naked blades? Leucippus long time since
To us betrothed these daughters, and to us
His oath confirmed this marriage. Yet with bribes—
Cattle and mules and other gifts—you stole
Our plighted brides, subverting shamefully
Their father's soul, and robbed us of our right.
Oft have I spoken, though not prone to speak,
Thus to your faces; "Heroes woo not so,
Good friends, nor steal brides vowed to other men.
Sparta is wide, horse-breeding Elis wide,
Arcadia rich in flocks, Achaea's towns,
Messene, Argos and the whole broad coast
Of Sisyphus; numberless maidens there
Dwell with their parents, lacking naught in grace
And character; not hard to choose of these
Whomso you will; world-famous heroes ye,
Heroes your fathers, your ancestral blood
Heroic; gladly such would many seek
To wed their daughters. Nay, my friends, let be;
These maids be ours, others be yours!" I spake
This and much else, but to the ocean waves
My words were borne away by the wind's breath
And all my pleas were vain. Hard-hearted both
And obstinate! Yet even now give ear;
Our sires are brothers and ourselves close kin!'

Castor   'If you would fight, pursue our mortal strife,
And steep our spears in fratricidal blood,
Let Lynceus and myself, the younger pair,
Submit our quarrel to the chance of war;
Let Idas and my brother stand aside
And fight not; so our sires may grieve the less.
One house to mourn one son—'twere loss enough!
Then those who live shall wed, while their dear friends
Make merry; and the end of strife be peace.'

So Castor spake and Heaven smiled on his words.
Idas and Polydeuces, elders both,
Unlaced their shoulder gear and set it down.
Into the midst, shaking his challenging spear
Beneath the shield's rim Lynceus, Castor too,
Brandishing lance-points, stepped; nodded the plume
On either crest; and first they toiled to strike
Where in the chinks of armour they espied
Some naked flesh; but ere the points went home
The dread shields caught and broke them; from the
sheath
Each drew his sword, eager to make an end.
No stay in the fight; on the broad shield and helm
Blow after blow dealt Castor, stroke on stroke
Keen-sighted Lynceus, and his blade's sharp edge
Near shore the crimson plume. Foiled, Lynceus strove
To strike his foe's left knee; but Castor swerved,
Recoiled, lopped off his fingers; stricken sore,
Lynceus let fall his sword, in haste to flee
Sped towards his father's tomb, where Idas lay
Watching the unnatural conflict, kin with kin.
Swift in pursuit the son of Tyndareus
Hastened, and with his sharp broad-bladed sword
Pierced side and navel; parted by the steel
Out gushed the bowels; there lay Lynceus prone
And on his eyelids fell the weight of sleep.

Yet at the ancestral hearth no marriage feast
Gladdened Laocoösa's eyes; for straight
Messenian Idas, tearing forth the stone
That crowned his father's tomb, was fain to fling
Its mass with fatal force on him who had slain
His brother; but the mighty arm of Zeus
Struck the wrought marble from the avenging hand
And burned the slayer with a bolt of fire.

Thus were it no light venture to defy
The sons of Tyndareus; for valiantly
They take the field, sons of a valiant sire.
Children of Leda, graciously inspire
Our hymns that all may spread their fame who hear.
And so farewell! To you all bards are dear,
To Helen too, and those by whose employ
Prince Menelaus sacked the towers of Troy.
Glory for you, O princes, and renown
Homer firm founded, when of Priam's town,
The Achaean fleet, the Ilian wars and bold
Achilles, warrior, tower of strength, he told.
I too what strains the clear-voiced Muses bring,
What tender strains, to enhance your glory sing,
And all of song my own poor store affords;
For gods such hymns are meetest of rewards.

IDYLL XXIII

THE LOVER

A lover pined for a beautiful boy
With a wayward mind; he took no joy
In a fond caress, and naught could move
Him to tenderness. He knew not love
Nor the wounding dart that the god can wield.
He would not speak; he would not yield
To the wild desire of his lover's heart;
No blushing cheek, no brightening eye
To quench the fire; no kiss, no sigh.
As wild beasts glare at the foe's advance
To their forest lair, with cruel glance
And insolent pride his lover he eyed,
And pale of hue his visage grew;

And yet so fair in his wrath he proved
That ever the more his lover loved.
No more could he bear love's pitiless flame
But weeping sore to the house he came
And cried aloud, 'Hard! Merciless!
For love unmeet! What lioness
Reared thee for brood? And now the last
Sad gift I bring—this halter! The way
That cures, men say, all ills of past
Remembering, I tread! 'Tis thou
Hast set my feet on the path of pain!
And no more now shall this passion of mine
Displease thee; yet, should I raise and drain
To the bitter lees oblivion's wine,
Can I e'er forget? I kiss thy door
And find my ease! For my sad heart knows
What lies in store. Fair is the rose
In the springtime day, but how soon its leaf
Will wither away! And fair is the bloom
On boyhood's cheek, but, alas, how brief!
And a time will come when thou shalt seek
With a heart on fire and vain desire
Thy love! One last kind deed, I pray,
Dear boy, be thine; when on thy way,
The threshold past, this body of mine
Thou seest swing before thy door,
Pass not, but stay, an offering
Of warm tears pay, and gently set
Thy raiment o'er my wretched corse!
One last embrace bestow; let this,
Thy lips' sweet grace, thy final kiss,
Pay the full debt of thy remorse!
Be not afraid! I can no more
Do thee despite! My corse be laid
With all its store of hidden love

In a hollow grave; and ere thou move
From my tomb, this rite perform, I crave;
Cry thrice, "Here one I love lies dead!"
And again, "My friend is gone, is gone!"
And on the stone above my head
Write, as I write upon thy wall,
"Love made an end of this poor wight!
Who pass this way, wayfarers all,
A moment stay and say, 'He found
A cruel friend!' "' Then on the ground
A stone he set; the fine cord's end
To the lintel bound, mounted and tied
The halter round his neck; aside
He spurned the stone and lifeless hung.
From the open door the boy espied
Where the body swung; no tear he shed
For the death new-done; by the touch of the dead
Sullied, unmoved, he ran to the game
And the baths he loved; at last he came
To the god whose grace he had scorned, and stepped
On the statue's base; from the pedestal leapt
To the water below; but Eros too
Sprang down and slew that heartless youth.
And the water was red with the blood of the dead,
And there echoed above the boy's faint voice,
'Rejoice, rejoice, ye lovers, in truth
In the power of love; for the hater is killed!
Ye that hate, learn ruth; for the god hath willed
Just doom on all who scorn his thrall!'

THE BOYHOOD OF HERACLES

Two babes there were, the elder, Heracles,
Of nigh one year; the other, Iphicles,
Born one night later. On an eve it fell
Alcmene, Midea's queen, who loved them well,
Tenderly bathed and set them to her breast
And laid them in the brazen shield to rest,
That burnished shield Amphitryon her lord
From Pterelaus, fallen to his sword,
Had seized; and as she stroked each tiny head,
Lulling her babes to rest, she softly said,
'Sweet dreams attend you! Sleep and wake again!
Sleep safe, my life, my soul, my children twain!
And happy be your slumber! Morning yield
You happiness!' She rocked the mighty shield
Till sleep embraced them.

                When at dead of night
The Bear turns west, and great Orion's light
Reveals his shoulder, through the latticed door
On the broad threshold of the palace floor
Did Hera, mistress of all crafts, impel
Two dread and monstrous snakes, hooded and fell,
With sinuous grey-blue coils, and bade them seize,
Seize and devour the infant Heracles.
Spitting foul poison, rippling coils unwound,
Fierce eyes ablaze with fire, along the ground
They writhed on murder bent; but when they crept
With flickering tongues nigh where the infants slept,
The queen's dear babes awoke; throughout the hall
Light flashed, the light of Zeus who knoweth all.

No sooner Iphicles the foul brutes spied
From out the hollow shield than, terrified
By the merciless teeth, he screamed and would have fled,
Kicking the woollen blanket from his bed.
But Heracles rose up and with bare hands
Met their assault, and as with steely bands
Gripped their two throats, where loathly serpents store
The deadly venom e'en great gods abhor.
Writhing, their coils the monstrous serpents wound
That nursling babe, who knew no tears, around;
But, forced by that unyielding grip, were fain
To slack their spines, striving to ease the strain.

First rose Alcmene, wakened by the cries;
'Up, up Amphitryon! Dear my lord, arise,
Nor stay for sandals! Haste thee, for affright
Benumbs my sense! See how at dead of night,
Illumined by mysterious rays, the walls,
As it were dawn, glow clear! Hark, through the halls
Loud rings our younger darling's scream! I ween
Here is some strange mishap!' So spake the queen.
Rose from his bed Amphitryon at her word,
Hasting distraught to seize the well-chased sword
That hung about his cedar couch; he sought
The carven sheath of lotus-wood well-wrought
And the new-woven sword-belt on the wall;
And sudden darkness filled the spacious hall.
Straight roused he then his thralls as slumbering
Deeply they breathed: 'Up, slaves, haste ye and bring
Light from the hearth! Unbolt the chamber door!'
And a Phoenician dame, who on the floor
By the corn-mill slept, cried loud, 'Rise up, ye thralls!
Rise, stout of heart! It is the master calls!'
Obedient to the summons, lamp ablaze,
This way and that they sped in swift amaze.

When they beheld the infant gripping tight
In tender hands those monsters, at the sight
They cried aloud; but the all-conquering boy
Held high the dreadful snakes and leapt for joy
And laughed as at his father's feet he laid
The vanquished brutes, self-glorying, unafraid.
But Iphicles the queen snatched to her breast,
Rigid with panic, whimpering, distressed.
Amphitryon raised the elder brother, spread
The lambs'-wool coverlet and sought his bed.

Thrice had the cocks proclaimed the dawning near
When the queen called Teiresias the seer,
Truth-teller; of this marvel strangely wrought
Bade him declare the issue: 'Hide me naught',
She cried, 'nor yet respect my royal state,
If Heaven portends disaster! All that Fate
Draws from her distaff mortals must abide.
Thou art a prophet; whatsoe'er betide,
Eueres' son, thou knowest, nor of me
Hast need for teacher.' To Alcmene's plea
Returned Teiresias, 'O Perseus' seed,
Thou who hast borne brave babes, take heart at need!
Prize in thy soul the best of what shall be!
As with her hand she rubs upon her knee
The soft spun yarn, full many an Argive dame
Shall praise at the evening's end Alcmene's name—
By the sweet light that long since fled mine eyes
I swear it—and so great a man shall rise
To the starry heaven, of broad heroic breast,
Lord of all beasts, of men the mightiest,
That women in all Greece shall celebrate
Thy glory and thy son's—a mother great,
A greater son; and next, as Fate decrees,
Twelve toils accomplished, he shall dwell at ease

With Zeus; his mortal part the funeral flame
Shall burn at Trachis; wedded, men shall name
Heracles son of that immortal pair
Who sped these murderous monsters from their lair.
Lay fire beneath the ash, and every kind
Of thorny shrub, dry, beaten by the wind,
Bramble or paliurus or wild pear,
Set on to burn; on that rough firewood there
Pile up these corpses at the midnight hour,
The hour when those vile creatures crept to devour
Thy babe. Then at the dawning give command
All ash be gathered by some maiden's hand,
Borne o'er the river to the broken screes
And cast away beyond our boundaries.
Let her return nor glance behind; the rooms
Shall first be smoked with sulphur's cleansing fumes;
Pure water mixed with salt—so runs the rule—
Sprinkled from foliage bound about with wool,
Shall next avert all evil; sacrifice
To Zeus a boar, that of your enemies
Ye may be ever lords as Zeus is Lord.'
So spake the age-worn seer, and with the word
Rose from his ivory seat and went his way.

Then like some tender sapling from that day
Grew 'neath his mother's loving care the son—
For so men called him—of Amphitryon
The Argive. Aged Linus, Phoebus' seed,
Vigilant guardian, taught the boy to read;
From Eurytus he learnt the archer's craft,
To bend the bow and flight the unerring shaft—
Eurytus, lord of broad ancestral lands;
Philammon's son, Eumolpus, set his hands
To pluck the boxwood lyre and taught the art
Of minstrelsy; Harpalycus for his part,

Phocian, Hermes' son, whose scowling brow
And truculent face, e'en from afar, would cow
The opponent in the arena, made him wise
In all those skills pancratiasts devise
Who fall full length and wrestle on the ground,
Tricks too that boxers know, whose leather-bound
Fists crush the adversary, the subtle trips
That Argives use, crook'd legs and twisting hips,
To throw the other; in the chariot-race
To handle steeds and at the turning-place
Guard the projecting nave, Amphitryon
Himself with loving wisdom trained his son.
Victor in contests, many a priceless meed
The king had brought from Argos, where men feed
The horses; and the chariots that he raced
Brake not until their time-worn straps unlaced.
With careful aim the lunging spear to wield,
His shoulder guarded 'neath the upraised shield,
To abide the sword-stroke, form the phalanx, gauge
The advancing foeman's force, prepare to engage
The foe with mounted men—such arts were taught
By Castor, Hippalus' son, whom exile brought
From Argos famed for steeds—whose wide estate
And vineyard passed to Tydeus, confiscate
By king Adrastus; warrior held in truth,
Till years had dulled the bloom of vigorous youth,
First among demigods, pre-eminent.

Such were the arts whereto his mother lent
Her loving guidance; by his father's side
A lion-skin was his couch, his joy and pride.
Roast flesh his evening meal and Dorian bread
Enough to send a labouring serf to bed
Well satisfied; yet would he break his fast
On frugal fare—a light uncooked repast.

And for his simple raiment Heracles
Wore but a tunic falling to the knees.

HERACLES AND THE RUSTIC

Then the old ploughman, watchman of the herd,
Stayed from his ploughing and made answer thus:

'Gladly, O stranger, all that thou would'st know
Will I declare; Hermes I reverence,
Lord of the Ways; great is his power and great
His wrath beyond the wrath of other gods
That falls on those who churlishly deny
Their aid to a questing traveller. Hark then;
Not all together graze the fleecy flocks
Of king Augeas, in one field or spot;
Some pasture on the banks of Helisous
And some by holy Alpheus' sacred stream,
Some by the vineyards of Buprasium,
Some here; and for each several flock a fold
Stands separate, but for his countless herds
Here by the broad expanse of Menius' lake
Are meadows ever green with pasturage.
For here the dewy fields and watered meads
Grow sweet abundance of lush herbs to stay
The strength of hornéd cattle; to thy right
Show plain their stalls, beyond the running stream,
There where the plane-trees and green olives grow
In plenty, holy shrine of that great god,
Apollo of the Pastures; close beside
See ranged the homesteads, where abide the hinds
Who guard with diligence the king's estate,

97

His vast and wondrous wealth, and cast the seed
On fallow ground, or three times turned or four.
The busy gardeners tend his boundaries
Where are the orchards, but at harvesting
Come in to help at the wine-vats; this whole plain,
Corn-bearing acres, wooded copses—all
Down to the spring-fed borderlands are his,
The estate of king Augeas; all day long
We labour on them—this our lot in life—
Husbandmen we, his serfs who dwell on the land.
But tell me now—for it will profit thee—
Whom would'st thou seek, Augeas or a serf?
I know and I will tell thee all I know.
For thou art noble and of noble birth,
Or so I judge, and thy strong limbs declare
The truth of it; e'en such as thou appear
Sons of immortals when they dwell with men.'

To whom replied the valiant son of Zeus:
'Yea, Augeas is he, Epean king,
Of whom I stand in need; to search him out
Hither I came; but if he bides awhile
In the town among his folk and seeks their weal,
To aid them in their judgements, then, old sir,
Lead on, that I may find that serving-man
Who wields the weightiest authority;
With him would I converse; it is God's will
One man should seek another's help in need.'

And thus the good old ploughman made reply:
'Surely, O stranger, 'tis some god hath urged
Thy coming hither, for with no delay
Thy need is met; for Helios' dear child,
With Phyleus, his great and valiant son,
Hath come but yesterday, leaving the town

After long time, to view his vast estates
That lie in the country; kings, like lesser folk,
Hold their possessions safer when themselves
Secure their interests; come then with me
To my steading, where belike he may be found.'

With that he led him on, but as he eyed
The lion's pelt and the weighty club he bore,
Pondering whence this stranger came, desired
To ask him; yet whene'er the unuttered word
Sprang to the threshold of his lips, would pause,
Fearing to cross his mood, so swift he strode.
When they drew near the old man's home, the hounds
By scent and sound quickly aware, from far
Rushed upon Heracles, Amphitryon's son,
Loud barking; from all sides they rushed to attack,
While still with silly whimpering they fawned
On the old ploughman, who with angry threats
And stones half-lifted drove them thence and checked
Their clamour, in his heart well satisfied
They should so guard their absent master's home.
'Dear heaven!' he cried. 'What a brute beast is this
And over-hasty that the immortal gods
Have given to be man's comrade! Were the wits
Within him keen, did he know friend from foe,
There's not a beast could equal him for worth;
But now his savage temper passes all!'
So came they swiftly to the old man's home.

Then Helios turned his steeds towards the west,
Bringing on evening, and the fat flocks came,
Leaving their pasture for the farms and folds.
Next in their myriads, herd on herd, the cows
Came on like watery clouds that in the heavens
Stream onward, driven by the south wind's blast

Or by the north from Thrace; so numberless,
So without pause they drive across the sky,
Crest after crest, wind-driven, cloud on cloud.
Countless as they, herd followed herd; the plain
And all the paths were thronged with their return,
And with the bellowing cattle the green fields
Were straitened; soon the kine with rolling gait
Came jostling to the stalls and in the folds
The sheep were penned. No man of all those hinds
Idled among the cattle, none lacked work.
One to his feet bound clogs with well-cut straps
Ready to milk close to the cows' warm flanks;
One set the calves beneath their mothers' teats,
Eager to drink the fresh warm milk; here one
Would hold a pail, another set rich cheese
And one part bulls from cows within the stalls.
And among all the sheds king Augeas
Moved to appraise the herdsmen's guardianship
Of his vast wealth, and with him went his son
And Heracles, resolute man of might,
Companying him to view his rich estate.
Then did Amphitryon's son, though firm his soul
Nor lightly shaken, watch in sheer amaze
Those myriad herds, marvellous gift from heaven.
For none would say nor in imagining
Deem it were possible one single lord—
Nor even ten, though wealthiest of all kings—
Should own such countless kine; with this great gift,
Surpassing wealth of cattle, Helios
Had dowered his son, himself so labouring
That all this stock should never waste but thrive.
No such distemper plagued the royal herds
As vainly wastes the herdsman's toil, but still
Yearly increased the hornéd kine and grew
More goodly, for, as did none other herd,

His cows bore heifers, calves that lived and throve.
Came with the cows three times a hundred bulls,
Black-skinned, white-thighed, and twice a hundred red,
All in their season ripe to mate; thereto
Twelve were there, consecrate to Helios,
That roved the pastures, swan-white, eminent
Mid all the cattle, and apart they grazed
The luscious herbage, glorying in their might.
When from their forest shelters savage beasts
Dashed to the plain to seize the grazing kine,
Swift scenting them those twelve would rush to attack,
Eyes flashing slaughter, bellowing threats; of these
Far first in might and strength and arrogance
Was the great Phaethon, likened to a star
By all the herdsmen, so pre-eminent,
So bright among the rest his splendid form.
No sooner Phaethon glimpsed the tawny hide
Of the glaring lion than he rushed to attack
The wary hero, lowering his strong brow
In act to crush his ribs; but straight the prince
Grasped in his hand the bull's left horn and stayed
His furious onslaught; down he bent the neck
For all its massive weight, down to the ground,
And with a shoulder-thrust forced the beast back.
Out bulged the muscles of his upper arm
Above the corded sinews. Augeas,
Phyleus, his prudent son, and all the hinds
Attendant on the kine beheld amazed
The might resistless of Amphitryon's son.

Phyleus and Heracles, that man of might,
Left the rich meadow-lands and sought the town,
Treading the narrow path that from the stalls
Passed through a vineyard barely seen for weeds.
Where first the highway met their hurrying feet,

Phyleus, dear son of Augeas, turned his head
And over his right shoulder thus addressed
Heracles, son of Zeus, who strode behind:
'Friend, many years ago I heard a tale—
Was it of thee?—that now I call to mind.
There passed this way from Helice by the sea
And Argos an Achaean; I was young;
He told a tale, how as he watched the scene
Some man of Argos slew a savage beast,
A monstrous lion, plague of the neighbourhood,
Whose lair was by the shrine of Nemean Zeus,
A hollow cavern; not to me alone
Told he this tale, to many an Epean too.
"Whether the slayer dwelt in Tiryns town,
In holy Argos or Mycenae, that
I know not rightly." So he testified;
But this I mind me, if my memory serves,
He said the hero was of Perseus' line.
No other Greek, I ween, but only thou,
Could venture such an exploit, and the hide
That hangs about thy shoulders doth proclaim
Right certainly the valiance of thy hands.
Tell me then, hero, first that I may know
If I guess truly, judge thyself aright,
Art thou that man of whom this tale was told,
Here as we heard it, by that traveller,
The man from Helice? This too declare,
How thou didst slay that deadly beast alone,
And how it came to Nemea's stream-fed land.
For no such portent in the Apian state,
Search as one might, could e'er be found; no brute
So huge can it sustain, but only bears,
Ravaging wolves and boars; thus those who heard
Were all astonished; slow to credit, some
Doubted the tale as feigned to please the ear.'

So Phyleus spake and, stepping from mid-path,
Made room for Heracles to walk beside,
That he might hear more clearly all he said.
And Heracles made answer: 'Augeas' son,
True thine unaided judgement; I am he.
This first; and for the rest how all befell
Hear thou, since 'tis thy will, save only this,
Whence came this monster: that no Argive knows,
Of all in the city none can tell; mayhap
(We do but guess) some god in jealous mood,
Vexed by some ritual fault, sent forth this curse
To plague the sons of Phoroneus. In truth,
Mercilessly, like a river in spate,
Ravished that brute the dwellers in the marsh,
Those of Bembina more than all, who dwelt
Nigh to his lair; unbearable their plight.
This labour first, at Eurystheus' behest,
I sought to accomplish; for he bade me slay
That fearful beast; so with my pliant bow
And hollow quiver filled with feathered shafts
I ventured forth, and in one hand a club
Cut from the spreading olive, all compact
Of bark and pith, found under Helicon
And torn from the earth, stock, matted roots entire.
Then when I came to where the lion lay,
I seized my bow and strung it to the notch,
Fitting thereto an arrow fraught with doom.
This way and that I glanced in hope to sight
The deadly monster ere he sighted me.
'Twas noon, nor yet could I trace out his prints
Nor hear his roar; nor in the cornfield's space
Was one to till the land or tend the kine
Whom I might question; every labourer
Stayed in his steading, prey to pallid dread.
Still I lay hid, scanning the tree-clad hill,

Till I should view the monster and prepare
To test my prowess on the sight; 'twas eve,
And now the beast, sated with flesh and blood,
Gore on his tangled mane, grim chops and chest,
Tongue licking jaws, made for his forest den.
In the shady thicket on the wooded track
Swiftly I crouched, waiting where he should pass;
And as he came, my barbed shaft I loosed
And struck his flank on the left; but all in vain
My arrow sped, nor could it pierce his hide
But back on the green grass fell. In fierce amaze
Raising his blood-splashed forehead from the ground,
All ways he glared to seek the hidden foe,
Baring teeth ravenous in open jaws.
Vexed with the event, a second shaft I sped
And where the lung lies struck the monster's chest;
Yet still in vain the pitiless arrow flew
And checked by that tough hide fell at his feet.

Grievously troubled, yet once more I raised
My bow in act to shoot when suddenly,
Rolling fierce eyes around, the merciless beast
Spied me and, coiling his long tail about,
Prepared for instant battle; furiously
Swelled his whole neck, bristled his tawny mane;
Back bow-like curved, crouching he made to spring.
As when some wheelwright, skilled in many a craft,
Heats and then bends the wild fig's well-cleft shoots,
To shape the chariot's felloes—all at once
The tough-barked wood springs from his hands and leaps
To a distance, even so the fearful brute,
Gathering his limbs together, from afar
Leapt on me, eager to devour my flesh.
Then from my back I snatched the double cloak,
Held it in front with arrows poised in hand

And, raising my stout cudgel in the air,
Crashed it amain on the brute's skull; and full
On that invulnerable shaggy head
Dashing it down split the tough wood in twain.
High in mid-air the lion checked, then fell
Down to the earth and stood on quivering feet,
Stunned by the shock, brain shattered in the skull,
And on both eyes a cloud of darkness fell.
So when I marked him all bewildered stand,
Grievously hurt, ere he should find his wits,
I seized the nape of that resistless neck,
Casting my bow and quiver to the ground.
Then from behind, lest he should rend my flesh
With his sharp claws, my strong hands choked his throat.
My heels were on his feet, firm pressed to earth;
My thighs controlled his flanks, till at the last
I raised him lifeless in my arms and stretched
His corpse upon the ground. The fight was done;
His spirit fled to the vast world of shades.
Then mused I long how from the dead beast's limbs
To strip the shaggy skin—hard task indeed;
For all my effort neither iron nor stone
Nor aught availed to cut it; but in the end,
Taught by some god, with his own claws I flayed
The lion swiftly then, and wrapped the hide
About me, guardian from the wounds of war.
So perished, friend, the Nemean brute, ere this
A curse on cattle and sore plague to man.

THE BACCHANALS

Three were the women, Ino, Agave
The white-cheeked, and the third, Autonoe,
Who to the sacred mountain led their bands
And, cutting foliage from the wild oak-tree
With ivy evergreen and asphodel
Low-growing, built with careful hands
Twelve altars—three for Semele
And nine for Dionysus on the open fell.

Then from the Chest the moulded offerings
They drew and laid the holy things
On their leaf-altars newly plucked, as he,
The god himself, had taught them, reverently
For his delight. But from a high rock, hidden
In an old mastich-bush, watcher unbidden,
Pentheus beheld the holy rites; and first
Autonoe spied him; from her wild lips burst
A fearful cry; sudden with hurrying feet
The sacred things of the frenzied god, unmeet
For profane gaze, she scattered—maddened she
And in a moment maddened all that company.

Panic-stricken Pentheus fled;
Belting tunics to the knee,
In hot pursuit the women sped.
'What would ye, Bacchanals, with me?'
He cried; to whom Autonoe,
'This shalt thou swiftly learn!'
'Why hear?' His mother, Agave,
Roared like a lioness with young
And bore away the severed head;

Ino, Autonoe in turn
This side and that, planting firm tread
Upon his belly, rent amain
From off his frame shoulder and shoulder-blade
While all the rest tore off and flung
From hand to hand raw flesh; e'en so their train
Came blood-besprinkled back to Thebes
And brought not Pentheus from the hill but Pain.

I care not; and for any foe
Of Bacchus let no other care,
Be he of tender years or know
More grievous pain than Pentheus bare.

May I be pure and all pure eyes delight;
Honoured the eagle in the high god's sight.
Pious the worshippers whose sons succeed
To happier lot, not so the impious breed.

Farewell to Bacchus, whom Lord Zeus the high
On snowy Dracanus from his glorious thigh
Released; farewell to beauteous Semele
And those Cadmean dames, her sisters three;
Full many a heroine reverences their name,
Whose deed, inspired by god, let no man blame.

IDYLL XXVII

A MAN AND A MAID

Girl   Once long ago clever Helen was ravished by Paris, a
                                            neatherd.
Daphnis Nay, Helen kissed him herself; 'twas her will to
                                            ensnare him with kisses.

G.   Don't you brag, little satyr! I kissed you—there's
                             nothing in kisses!

D.   Nothing in kisses indeed! Even meaningless kisses
                             are blissful!

G.   Faugh! I wipe my mouth and spit out the kiss that
                             you gave me!

D.   Wipe your mouth, do you? Come, give it here once
                             more and I'll kiss it!

G.   Keep your kisses for calves of your herd—they're not
                             for a maiden.

D.   Don't you brag! your youth's but a dream, running
                             swift to its ending.

G.   What if the dream runs on? Just now milk and honey's
                             my portion.

D.   Grapes of today are raisins anon; wither roses and
                             perish.

G.   Hands off, you! I'll scratch your lips if you come
                             any nearer!

D.   Come to the wild-olive grove and I'll tell you a story
                             will please you.

G.   No, that I won't! You beguiled me before with your
                             sweet little stories!

D.   Come with me then to the shade of the elms and hark
                             to my piping.

G.   Please your own self with your piping—it's dull to
                             my ears and I hate it!

D.   Fie! Even you, my girl, must beware of the wrath of
                             the Goddess.

G.   Goddess go hang! My trust is in Artemis; she will
                             defend me.

D.   Hush, lest the Paphian smite and you fall in her toils
                             and escape not!

G.   Smite as she will, I care not; for Artemis' favour
                             protects me.

D. Nay, but you cannot flee Love; never yet has a
                                    maiden escaped him.
G. Yes, by Pan, I'll escape him; but you—may he bind
                                    you for ever!
D. Men there are worser than I, and I fear he may find
                                    you a worser.
G. Suitors in plenty have wooed me—as yet never one
                                    to my liking.
D. Here's yet another! 'Tis I, one more of the many to
                                    woo you.
G. What shall I do, my friend? There's trouble in wedding
                                    and sorrow.
D. Trouble and sorrow in wedding? A wedding's the
                                    season for dancing.
G. Wives, so they say, live in terror and dread of
                                    tyrannical husbands.
D. Nay, not so; it's the wives are the tyrants! What
                                    reason to fear then?
G. Child-birth's pangs are a terror; how keen are the
                                    shafts of the Goddess!
D. Artemis lightens the pains, whom you claim for a
                                    royal protector.
G. Yes, but I fear, if I bear, I may ruin my beauty in
                                    bearing.
D. In the dear babes that you bear your youth's new
                                    dawn will be breaking.
G. Say, what gift do you bring if I come to you, worth
                                    the surrender?
D. You shall be mistress of all my glades, my pasture and
                                    oxen.
G. Swear, if I wed you, you'll never desert me unless I
                                    should will it.
D. Nay, though you drive me away, by Pan, I'll never
                                    desert you.

G.   Then will you build for your bride a chamber, a house
          and a steading?

D.   Surely I'll build you a chamber, and fairly your flocks
          will be pastured.

G.   Oh, but my aged father! What, what sort of tale can I
          tell him?

D.   Let him but hear my name and the news of your
          troth will delight him.

G.   Tell me the name that you bear, for the sound of a
          name is a pleasure.

D.   Daphnis am I, my sire Lycidas and my mother
          Nomaea.

G.   Well-born truly, but I come of stock not unworthy
          to match you.

D.   That I know; Acrotime's your name and your father's
          Menalcas.

G.   Come now, show me your wood—the glade that
          shelters the farmstead.

D.   Come this way then and see my slender cypresses
          growing.

G.   Browse, my goats; I'm away to the farm of Daphnis
          the neatherd.

D.   Feed your fill, my bulls, while I show my glades to
          the maiden.

G.   What are you up to, you satyr? Why thrust your hand
          in my bosom?

D.   Delicate apples your breasts! First lessons I'll teach
          them in loving!

G.   Pan! I am fainting! Enough! Take out that hand from
          my garment!

D.   Courage, maid of my heart! Why tremble you, shy
          little darling?

G.   Now you're throwing me into the stream and my
          dress is all dirty.

D.   Look, here's a soft goatskin; I'll lay it beneath to
                                           protect you.

G.   Alas and alas for my girdle! You've torn it! Oh, why
                                    did you loose it?

D.   This is the first of the gifts that I offer the goddess
                                      of Paphos.

G.   Stop it, you wretch! There's a sound in the wood!
                            There's somebody coming!

D.   Only the cypresses telling each other the maiden is
                                     wedded.

G.   Now my wrap is in rags and I haven't a shred on my
                                        body!

D.   Take no thought for the wrap; I'll give you another
                                and ampler.

G.   You're all promises now, and tomorrow you'll grudge
                                 me a relish.

D.   Add to the gifts that I pledge my soul, were I able to
                                 pledge it.

G.   Artemis, be not wroth with a maid no longer a pupil!

D.   Duly I'll offer a heifer to Love and a cow to the
                                   Paphian.

G.   Maiden I came to the wood but a wife I return to the
                                homestead.

D.   Mother and wife and a nurse of babes—no longer a
                                  maiden.

Thus as they lay upon their stolen couch,
Delighting in their young limbs, each to each
They whispered, till at last with shamefast eyes
But happy heart she rose to tend her sheep
And he his oxen, joying in his bride.

Take now once more the pipe that doth belong
To thee, O happy herd, that we may hear
Another pastoral song
To please our listening ear.

THE DISTAFF

O ivory distaff, thou the spinners' friend,
   Grey-eyed Athene's gift to women wise
In housecraft, fearlessly my voyage attend
   To where the Cyprian's verdant precinct lies
   Amid soft rushes; there to glad my eyes
And a glad welcome find we sail; for there
   In Nereus' glorious town the friend I prize,
Nicias, dwells. Be this, O Zeus, my prayer
That favouring winds may speed us to the land
   Of that rare son of the melodious Three;
     Then shall I place thee, distaff, fashioned fair
Of ivory, to grace his lady's hand,
   That she may spin abundant thread with thee
     For men's fine dress and women's graceful wear.

Would that the shepherds in the fields would shear
   Their flocks of their soft fleeces to content
Slim-ankled Theugenis twice in the year,
   So busy she, so ever provident.
   Never to one less strong, less diligent,
Distaff, wrought in that land which is my own,
   Native to Syracuse, would I present
Thee, for thy home is that illustrious town
Founded by Ephyran Archias of yore,
   Of the Trinacrian isle world-famous heart.
     Now in Miletus shalt thou spend thy days,
Where Nicias dwells, skilled in all healing lore,
   And among wives exalt his lady's art
     And call to mind the friend who sings her praise.

And men will say, 'Small gifts great friendship prove;
Precious the offerings made by friends who love.'

TO A BOY (i)

'Truth in the cups' men say, dear youth;
So we who drink must speak the truth,
And I my inmost thoughts impart;
Thou lov'st me not with all thy heart.
I know it; half my life is mine,
The rest is vain; the fault is thine,
Who art so lovely. Dost comply?
The Blessed no more blest than I.
Dost thou deny me? Dark the day
As darkest night. Thus to betray
A loving heart were deadly wrong!
Boy, I am old and thou art young;
Heed then my counsel; so shalt thou
Thank me hereafter, profit now.
Build thou upon one tree one nest;
So shall no creeping thing molest
Thy quiet home; each day to perch
On different boughs and ever search
New branches—these were fickle ways!
Doth one scarce met behold and praise
Thy beauty? He's a friend long known;
The love that loved thee first, outgrown.
Heed me, and honoured shalt thou be;
Love will deal tenderly with thee,
Love, tamer of men's souls, whose art
Has robbed of steel my powerless heart.
By thy soft lips I pray thee, bear
In mind, the passage of one year
Cheats thee of one year's youth; apace
Comes ruthless age, the wrinkled face.
Youth past returns not; youth wears wings

Upon his shoulders; flying things
Are hard to capture; so be kind,
Kinder for this thou hast in mind.
Guileless return my guileless love.
When bearded cheeks thy manhood prove,
We may swear friendship, as of yore
Patroclus and Achilles swore.
Now would I seek, thy whim to please,
The apples of Hesperides;
Now ravish from Hell's portal dread
Cerberus, guardian of the dead;
But if thou bid the heedless wind
Bear off my words, with thoughts unkind,
Then, should'st thou call me at the door,
All passion spent, I'd come no more!

IDYLL XXX

TO A BOY (ii)

Alas, this heavy sickness, curst unease!
    The boy is not so fair—and yet all charm;
Sweetly he smiles; and so without surcease
    Two months a feverish love disturbs my calm.
Three days I suffer torment, then a space
    The ill abates; but—it was yesterday—
Passing, too shy to look me in the face,
    He reddened, quickly glanced, and looked away.
Ah, now no respite! Love denies me rest,
    Gripping my heart with tighter bonds; so home,
Nursing new pain in my fresh-wounded breast,
    I turned my steps, and to my soul said, 'Come,
Not done with yet? Put off these foolish ways!
    Hast thou forgot grey hairs are on thy head?

His feet are on the threshold of his days;
    Be wise and act not so; thy youth has fled!
This too remember—better hold aloof
    In age from love whose latter end is pain;
For him life speeds upon the swift deer's hoof;
    Tomorrow he'll cast loose and sail again.
Flowers his sweet youth among his youthful peers;
    For thee but memories and heart's desire
And torturing dreams recurrent through the years,
    Sufficing not—not one—to quench love's fire.'
So spake I to my soul in sad distress,
    Who then made answer, 'Would'st thou vanquish Love,
That crafty schemer? Easier far to guess
    How many nines number the stars above!'
Now, willing or unwilling, must I bow
    My neck to that god's yoke and serve him still,
Whose mighty power in ancient times brought low
    Zeus and the Cyprian goddess; such his will.
So with his lightest breath he lifts and bears
    Swiftly upon the wind and whirls away
My passionate heart, even as sportive airs
    A withered leaf that lives but for a day.

BION

LAMENT FOR ADONIS

'Alas for Adonis!' I cry. 'Dead is Adonis the fair!'
    And the Loves too cry, 'Alas! Adonis the fair is dead!'
    Awake, Cypris, awake! No more on thy bright-hued bed
Sleep! Beat thy breast, dark-robed; to the listening world
                                   declare,
Poor Cypris, 'Dead, alas, dead is Adonis the fair!'
    'Alas for Adonis!' I cry, and the Loves mourn Adonis dead!

There on the hills lies Adonis the fair, and the dark blood drips
   From the wound on the snow-white thigh, where the wild
                              boar's tusk dealt death—
   White thigh, white tusk—and the gentle sigh of his passing
                              breath,
How sad a sigh for Cypris! The rose has fled his lips,
And his eyes grow dim in death; dying the kiss on his mouth
   That Cypris fain would press—the last, though still she would
                              fain
      Kiss her beloved's corpse again and yet again;
But her kisses fall unaware on the lips of the dying youth.

'Alas for Adonis!' I cry, and the Loves mourn Adonis dead.
   Deep the wound in his thigh, the wound in her heart more
                              deep.
   Hark to the plaint of the hounds he loves! The Oreads weep
And the Cyprian goddess unbinds her locks; uncomforted,
Unkempt and barefoot about the forest glades she roves,
   Torn by the briers that gather the flow of her sacred blood,
   Crying aloud as she flies on her course through the endless
                              wood,
Calling in vain on her lord, in vain on the boy she loves.

Deep on his navel there lies the red blood's floating mass;
   From his wounded thigh to his breast crimson the once fair
                              skin,
   And the nipples, once so white, wax now incarnadine.
'Alas, Cytherea, alas!' cry the Loves; 'alas and alas!'

Lost is her fair young lord, and her beauty divine is lost;
   Fair was the Cyprian once with her living love by her side;
   Alas, with the death of her love Cytherea's beauty died!
The lament, 'Woe, woe for Cypris!' from hill to hill is tossed,
And the oaks in the forest cry, 'Alas for Adonis the fair!'
   The rivers too shed tears for Aphrodite; weep

The springs that flow from the hills for Adonis' last long sleep,
And for grief the flowers flush red, and the glades and the glens
declare
On Cythera's isle Cytherea's woe, 'Adonis is dead!
Adonis the fair is dead!' And Echo cries again,
'Dead is Adonis the fair!' Who would not weep amain
The sad sad tale of the Cyprian's love and her lover fled?

When she beheld and marked the flow from his wasting thigh,
The purple flow unstanched, with lifted hands she cried,
'Stay, my Adonis, stay till I lie by thy wounded side,
Hold thee for one last kiss! Awake, awake, nor die
Till I press my lips on thine! Breathe out thy living breath
Into my mouth, and thy spirit into my widowed heart,
That so I may drink to the full thy love ere yet we part,
Thou to Acheron's stream and the hateful king of Death!
Ah! wretched I! Thou fleest—I cannot follow thee,
Doomed as a goddess to live! But the kiss that he gave shall
be mine,
Cherished and guarded for ever! Take him, O Queen divine,
Take thou Adonis, my lord, if thou wilt, Persephone,
Mightier far than I! For all that is fair must flee
To thine arms, while I endure sorrow insatiate,
Lament Adonis dead, and fear thee, desolate!
O love, my love, thou diest, and my dear love for thee
Has taken wings like a dream; widowed and lost am I
And the Loves in my bower lie idle; the girdle I loose no
more
For my lover lost! Oh why, too daring, vie with a boar?
Wert mad?' So mourned Cytherea, and the Loves re-echoed
her cry,
'Alas, Cytherea, alas! Adonis the fair is dead!'
Tears from the Paphian's eyes and blood from Adonis' side
Flow on the soil, and there spring sweet flowers where
Adonis died—

Anemones pale for her tears, for his blood wild roses red.

'Alas for Adonis dead, Adonis the fair!' I weep.
  Now in the woods, Cytherea, mourn not for thy lord; no
                                            bed
  Fit for thy love are the lonely leaves; let Adonis dead
Lie as in life on thy couch, lovely as one asleep.
Now on the couch let him lie, the couch of beaten gold,
  Wrapt in the softest of coverlets, there where the sheltering
                                      night
  Shadowed thee clasped in thy lover's arms, till the wakening
                                      light
Called thee from hallowed dreams; for even the couch that of
                                      old
Summoned Adonis in life cries now for Adonis dead.
  Cast on him garlands and flowers! So wither the flowers
                                    as he!
  Pour on him unguents and scents! So perish they all, as for
                                    thee
The sweetness of thy life's perfume, Adonis thy love, is fled!

There lies thy delicate lover in covers of purple and red;
  There all about him the sorrowful Loves with tresses shorn
  Weep and fling last love-tokens to honour the lord they
                                  mourn—
Arrows, a bow, a feather, a quiver; and at his head
One stands fanning the boy with his wings, and others bear
  In a golden bowl water to lave his wounded thigh;
  One has loosened his sandal; and all the sad Loves cry,
'Alas, Cytherea, alas! Dead is Adonis the fair!'

Hymen has quenched every torch at the door and scattered the
                                  wreath,
  Scattered the bridal wreath! No more do we hear the refrain,
  'Hymen O Hymenaeus!' 'Adonis!' once and again

'Woe for Adonis!' his song; and the Graces mourn his death,
Weeping for Cinyras' son, and keener the cry they raise,
   One to another lamenting, 'Dead is the beauteous youth!'
   Than when they sang his praises; and even the Fates show
                                                              ruth,
   Wailing, 'Adonis! Adonis'. No heed Adonis pays,
Though the Fates sing spells to restore him; fain would
                                                the dead boy hear,
   But the Maid will not loose him. Enough, Cytherea, have
                                                done for the day
   With grief and tears; beat not thy breast; for a season stay!
Sorrow will come again with the fall of another year!

LOVE AND THE FOWLER

A fowler boy in a wooded grove
   Was snaring birds when on a tree
Perched mid the boughs he noted Love
   Half-hidden; overjoyed was he
      To mark so fine a prey.
Then swift he fitted rod to rod
   To lime the lovely bird; aware
But feigning fear, the wingéd god
   Hopped here, hopped there and mocked the snare.
      In anger and dismay
The boy threw down his rods and sought
   An ancient ploughman; vexed he cried,
'My art, old master, thou hast taught;
   See now where teasing Love doth hide;
      In vain my fowler's skill!'
The old man smiled and wagged his head;
   'Seek not to snare him! Flee this bird!
Herein lies happiness', he said,
   'To shun such prey; for, mark my word,

Dear boy, success bodes ill!
When thou to man's estate art grown,
  This bird that mocks the craft I taught
Will of a sudden flutter down
  And light upon thy head unsought!'

MASTER AND PUPIL

As I lay dreaming,
  I saw before me stand
  Great Aphrodite, and in her fair hand
She led boy Love reluctant seeming,
Eyes on the ground. 'Take him', she said,
  'Teach him to sing and play,
  Dear shepherd!' And so went her way.
Foolish, I thought him pupil, but instead
I found him master; all my rustic lore—
  How sweet Apollo framed the lute,
  Hermes the lyre, Athene's skill the flute
And Pan the flageolet—all this and more
I taught him; yet he paid no heed,
  Though earnestly I strove,
  But he would sing his little songs of love
And tell me tales of many a deed
By his dear mother wrought
  And fatal loves of gods and men.
  Ah! from my memory then
Vanished the lessons I had taught,
  And in their stead
  Love's little love-songs only were rememberéd.